Anxiety and Phobic Disorders

Disorders

A Pragmatic Approach

Clinical Child Psychology Library

Series Editors: Michael C. Roberts and Annette M. La Greca

ANXIETY AND PHOBIC DISORDERS
A Pragmatic Approach
Wendy K. Silverman and William M. Kurtines

PARENT–CHILD INTERACTION THERAPY
Toni L. Hembree-Kigin and Cheryl Bodiford McNeil

SEXUALITY
A Developmental Approach to Problems
Betty N. Gordon and Carolyn S. Schroeder

Anxiety and Phobic Disorders

A Pragmatic Approach

Wendy K. Silverman and
William M. Kurtines
Florida International University
Miami, Florida

Plenum Press • New York and London

Library of Congress Cataloging-in-Publication Data

Silverman, Wendy K.
    Anxiety and phobic disorders : a pragmatic approach / Wendy K.
Silverman and William M. Kurtines.
        p.   cm. -- (Clinical child psychology library)
    Includes bibliographical references and index.
    ISBN 0-306-45226-X (hardbound). -- ISBN 0-306-45227-8 (pbk.)
    1. Anxiety in children. 2. Phobias in children.   I. Kurtines,
William M. II. Title. III. Series.
    [DNLM: 1. Anxiety Disorders--in infancy & childhood. 2. Anxiety
Disorders--diagnosis. 3. Anxiety Disorders--therapy.   WM 172 S587a
1996]
RJ506.A58S55 1996
618.92'85223--dc20   96-4862
                                                                   CIP

ISBN 0-306-45226-X (Hardbound)
ISBN 0-306-45227-8 (Paperback)

© 1996 Plenum Press, New York
A Division of Plenum Publishing Corporation
233 Spring Street, New York, N. Y. 10013

10 9 8 7 6 5 4 3 2 1

Printed in the United States of America

In memory of my father, Nathan

—WKS

Foreword

For many years, anxiety and phobic disorders of childhood and adolescence were ignored by clinicians and researchers alike. They were viewed as largely benign, as problems that were relatively mild, age-specific, and transitory. With time, it was thought, they would simply disappear or "go away"—that the child or adolescent would magically "outgrow" them with development and that they would not adversely affect the growing child or adolescent. As a result of such thinking, it was concluded that these "internalizing" problems were not worthy or deserving of our concerted and careful attention—that other problems of childhood and adolescence and, in particular, "externalizing" problems such as conduct disturbance, oppositional defiance, and attention-deficit problems demanded our professional energies and resources. These assumptions and assertions have been challenged vigorously in recent years. Scholarly books (King, Hamilton, & Ollendick, 1988; Morris & Kratochwill, 1983) have documented the considerable distress and misery associated with these disorders, while reviews of the literature have demonstrated that these disorders are anything but transitory; for a significant number of youth these problems persist into late adolescence and adulthood (Ollendick & King, 1994). Clearly, such findings signal the need for treatment programs that "work"—programs that are effective in the short term and efficacious over the long haul, producing effects that are durable and generalizable, as well as effects that enhance the life functioning of children and adolescents and the families that evince such problems.

In this context, Wendy Silverman and Bill Kurtines present their treatment-oriented book, *Anxiety and Phobic Disorders: A Pragmatic Approach*. The basic premise of this book is, of course, its emphasis on pragmatism. Pragmatism represents both an attitude about treatment and an approach toward determining and implementing treatments that work. As they succinctly note, the pragmatic therapist "does what is useful and what works" (p. 11). The pragmatic therapist is guided by a problem-solving approach that examines problems such as anxiety and phobias in the rich contexts in which they are embedded and that selects treatments that work from a diversity of theoretical viewpoints in order to resolve or at least ameliorate these problems. Thus, both a pragmatic and contextualist approach is recommended by Silverman and Kurtines. The bulk of this book explicates and illustrates this approach in the assessment and treatment of these difficult and frequently refractory problems. Consistent with their point of view, Silverman and Kurtines acknowledge that the procedures they recommend might not be effective or efficacious with all youth who present with such problems; in such instances, they recommend a return to their contextualistic and pragmatic problem-solving approach to select and implement (or, in some cases, design) treatments that do work.

Silverman and Kurtines have done a major service to professional clinicians working with youth and their families by writing this book and sharing with us their rich insights and clinical acumen. For the practicing clinician, there is much to offer. Clear guidelines for selecting and using major assessment devices and treatment procedures are presented. In addition, verbatim transcripts of actual cases illustrate how and when to use these various strategies, as well as how to problem solve when "blocks" or obstacles are encountered in the assessment or treatment process. The book is, however, much more than a handbook or "cookbook." It instructs us in how to use the pragmatic, contextual approach and how to solve problems that we will inevitably encounter in our own clinical practices. For many of us, our practices will be enhanced as a result of reading this book and using the recommendations contained therein.

The authors have also presented a considerable challenge to the research community. Their emphasis on "treatments that work" goes against the grain of many of our long-held beliefs that effective and efficacious treatments must be wedded to, and presumably derived from, well-defined and articulated theories. We might ask, for example, whether treatments that borrow from such diverse theories as psychodynamic theory and social learning theory can be truly integrated into a viable treatment plan. Would not, at least in some instances, the tenets of these theories conflict and predict different treatment or assessment strategies? Do not some strategies or procedures based on theory "work" better than others? Defining "treatments that work" is, of course, a contentious issue at this time (Chambless, 1995), and one that is not easily resolved. Silverman and Kurtines are to be commended for presenting us with this fascinating challenge. The ball is in our court.

In sum, this is an excellent book. Clinicians and researchers alike will be stimulated by its crisp and penetrating analysis of the "realities" of treating anxious and phobic children and adolescents. We have ignored these youth for far too long; they deserve our concerted attention and energies. It is comforting to know that seasoned clinicians and researchers such as Silverman and Kurtines are addressing the problems of these youth and their families. They are in good hands.

Thomas H. Ollendick
Virginia Polytechnic Institute
and State University
Blacksburg, Virginia

REFERENCES

Chambless, D. (1995). Training in and dissemination of empirically validated psychological treatments: Report and recommendations. *The Clinical Psychologist, 48,* 3–23.

King, N. J., Hamilton, D. I., & Ollendick, T. H. (1988). *Children's phobias: A behavioural perspective.* Chichester: John Wiley & Sons.

Morris, R. J., & Kratochwill, T. R. (1983). *Treating children's fears and phobias: A behavioral approach.* New York: Pergamon Press.

Ollendick, T. H., & King, N. J. (1994). Diagnosis, assessment, and treatment of internalizing problems in children: The role of longitudinal data. *Journal of Consulting and Clinical Psychology, 62,* 918–927.

Preface

This book is addressed to students and professionals in the mental health field who work with children who suffer from excessive fear and anxiety. In this book we share with you some of our ideas about what you can do to enhance the quality of life for these children and their families. Our ideas about how treatment can be used to help children were refined as part of a program of therapy and clinical research that has been evolving at the Child and Family Psychosocial Research Center at Florida International University in Miami. The center grew out of our earlier efforts to address the problem of developing effective interventions for use with internalizing problems in children and adolescents. The center is comprised of a number of programs and laboratories and provides multifaceted child and family interventions that include both outpatient and community-based services. The center has been actively involved in formulating and articulating systematic and broad-based approaches to all types of interventions with youth and families, including both prevention and treatment.

The techniques and procedures for helping anxious children described in this book were refined as part of the activities of the Childhood Anxiety and Phobia Program (CAPP) at the center. Within the center, CAPP has the distinctive mission of developing and evaluating approaches to assessment and intervention specific to the phobic and anxiety disorders of youth. CAPP is currently conducting two projects involved in the development of this intervention funded by the National Institute of Mental Health (#44781 and #49680), with other grant applications under review or preparation for projects that seek to extend and refine this intervention.

CAPP's goal of developing interventions targeted at internalizing youth and their families emerged from a persistent problem in the literature that has considerable implications for both practitioners and researchers: Because children and adolescents with externalizing disorders are likely to have a direct and disruptive effect on the lives of other individuals and institutions, these are the youth who have been more likely to be referred to mental health professionals, and who have thus been the primary focus of research attention. As a consequence, our conceptual and practical knowledge pertaining to internalizing problems of youth lagged far behind. Only recently have children with internalizing problems, particularly anxiety and fear problems, become a primary interest of psychosocial intervention researchers.

In this book we share with you some ideas about how to help these troubled children. The book will provide you with an introduction to our "transfer-of-control" treatment approach and a practical, detailed description of how we use this transfer-of-control approach to implement our exposure-based treatment program with children with anxiety and phobic disorders.

In addition to providing clinically useful information about working with children, this book will also provide you with another type of information—information that will prove useful beyond working with children with anxious and phobic disorders. This book will introduce you to a broader perspective that we have found useful in organizing our thinking about all of the issues that we, as mental health professionals, face in our efforts to work with people in distress. This perspective, which is pragmatic in orientation, has helped to organize the way that we, as therapists, think about the clinical issues that we face in implementing our treatment approaches. It also has helped to organize the way that we, as clinical researchers, think about the research issues that we face in evaluating these treatment approaches.

We have, as a consequence, found this pragmatic perspective to have implications that extend beyond working with children with anxious and phobic disorders. This perspective offers a way of thinking about human behavior and development that we have found useful in our work with all types of people experiencing all types of distress. It has served to define the "attitude" that we as therapists bring to all of our efforts to work with people in distress. This book is therefore intended to be more than a "how-to" book or a "cookbook" for treating children with anxious and phobic disorders. It is intended to do more than explain and illustrate techniques and procedures. It will offer you a fresh perspective on helping troubled children that has implications for the broader orientation that you, as a mental health clinician or researcher, adopt in all your professional activities.

The book is organized into four parts. Part I, *Background*, introduces you to the perspective, the pragmatic "attitude," that makes up the broader framework for our basic treatment approach. Part II, *Evaluation*, describes some of the ways that we have found our pragmatic attitude to be useful in addressing the problem of assessing anxiety and phobic disorders in children. Part III, *Treatment*, describes our basic transfer-of-control approach for implementing an exposure-based treatment program with children with anxiety and phobic disorders. Although the transfer-of-control approach that we describe is applicable to both children and adolescents, adaptation would be necessary for the very young child or for the older adolescent. In this book, our focus is on applying the model with elementary- and middle-school-age children. Part IV, *New and Better Ways*, describes some of the ways that we have extended our basic treatment approach to include working with other problems, populations, and contexts.

This book would not have been possible without the help of the children and the families with whom we have worked over the years. We express our deepest gratitude to them—and the strength and wisdom they have shared with us. We also wish to thank the editors of the series, Michael Roberts and Annette La Greca, for their thorough and constructive review of the manuscript that preceded this book. We also want to thank the editorial staff at Plenum Press for their patience and all our other colleagues and students for their help throughout the various stages of the book. Finally, we thank our families—Effie, Daniel, and Rachel, and Heather and Robyn—for being sources of support for us through both anxious and nonanxious times.

Wendy K. Silverman and William M. Kurtines

Contents

IV. New and Better Ways

Background

A Pragmatic Attitude

> *No particular results then, so far, but only an attitude of orientation, is what the pragmatic method means. The attitude of looking away from first things, principles, "categories," supposed necessities; and of looking toward last things, fruits, consequences, facts.*
>
> —*William James, 1907*

Marie, an 11-year-old female, was referred to our center for treatment by a school counselor because of periodic episodes of school refusal, excessive social withdrawal, and an extreme need for reassurance. When her mother brought her in for treatment, she described Marie as being "scared of everything." Even such an ordinary thing as going to sleep at night was a major event—her mother had to stay with Marie in her room until the girl fell asleep. She said that ever since she could remember Marie was different from other kids in this type of excessive fearfulness, timidity, and her constant need for reassurance. Marie, she said, spent a lot of time worrying about little things and making these little things into big things. She worried about her grades even though she was just finishing the year as an "A" student in a gifted program. In fact, her mother said, she wouldn't be surprised if Marie spent this summer as she did last summer—worrying about the teacher she'll get in the fall.

When the therapist talked to her, Marie was initially quiet and compliant and said very few words. She began by describing how she often has trouble falling asleep at night because she is afraid that burglars might break in and kidnap her and kill her family. She talked about recent burglaries in the neighborhood and about the missing children whose pictures are on milk cartons. She talked about how much this worried her. Although her initial focus was on personal security and safety, as she began to warm up to the therapist it became clear that her worries and fears were much more pervasive, and that they had an extensive impact on the quality of her life as well as that of her family.

Marie's worries dominated her life. She worried a lot about what other people thought of her, especially other kids. At school, she even worried about having to walk up to the front of the classroom to throw scrap paper into the wastebasket because the other kids would look at her. Being evaluated by her teacher for anything was even more painful. After school, she spent most of her time at home with her mother and did not like to be away from her. She rarely had anything to do with other children outside of school.

Marie's worries were extremely disruptive for her family. Many "everyday" family activities were prohibitive because of her worries. Going to restaurants, for example, was out of the question because Marie felt uncomfortable eating in public. Family conflicts were arising as a result of Marie's worries. Although Marie's parents had grown accustomed to changing family plans and routines so that Marie would not have to face things that made her feel anxious, they were beginning to feel angry and resentful. They wanted to go to restaurants every now and then! A particular area of conflict related to Marie's nighttime fears. Marie's mother was very tired of having to stay in her daughter's room for at least one hour every night at bedtime, until Marie fell asleep. It deprived her of her own greatly needed "alone time" with her husband—time for just the two of them, without the children.

These are the types of problems that all therapists who work with children commonly see. The specific areas of concern may not be exactly like Marie's; the areas may be more pervasive than Marie's or they may be less. They are, however, problems that cause extreme duress and suffering in many children. Large numbers of these children are so preoccupied with excessive, troublesome thoughts and feelings that they are unable to engage in many common activities—activities that may involve the family, the peer group, or the school. By not engaging in such activities, additional areas of difficulty and impairment usually arise. In Marie's case family conflict and impaired peer relationships arose. In other cases, academic failure, self-esteem difficulties, and other related problems may ensue.

As mental health professionals we recognize that the types of excessive and interfering thoughts, feelings, and behaviors that cause these children distress are problems that are diagnosed as anxiety and phobic disorders. These are children of great concern, and as mental health professionals our concern is about what can we do to help them.

Evidence is accumulating that anxiety and phobic disorders are highly prevalent among children and adolescents. Depending on the type of disorder and method of assessment employed, prevalence rates have been estimated as ranging between 1% to 17% (e.g., Kashani & Orvaschel, 1988; McGee et al., 1990). These rates reflect youth who have anxiety and phobic conditions severe enough to impair their daily functioning. For example, a proportion of these youth may be unable to attend school, to interact with peers, or to stay alone in bed at night. A sizable segment of these children and adolescents require professional help to improve their functioning and to alleviate the psychological distress associated with excessive anxiety and fear.

The long-term costs of *not* intervening are high. Many of the associated problems of childhood anxiety disorders such as excessive school absenteeism and impaired peer relations have been linked with later developmental problems (e.g., school drop-out, inadequate vocational adjustment, self-concept problems). In addition, although longitudinal data on childhood anxiety disorders are sparse, existing evidence coupled with retrospective reports of adults with anxiety and phobic disorders suggests some continuity between child and adult disorders (e.g., Abe, 1972; Ost, 1987). Many adult patients report being anxious or fearful "all their lives" or "as long as they can remember." Finally, youth and their parents expend considerable time and energy in the treatment process (e.g., Kazdin, 1993). An estimated $1.5 billion is being spent each year on treating children with "mental disorders" (Institute of Medicine, 1989), a proportion of which goes for treating childhood anxiety and phobic disorders.

In this book we share with you some ideas about how to help these troubled children. The chapters that follow will provide you with a wealth of clinically useful information specifically about treating children with anxious and phobic disorders. The chapters will include a brief outline of our basic "transfer-of-control" treatment approach, and a practical, detailed description of how we use this transfer of control approach to implement our exposure-based procedures that target maladaptive behavioral, cognitive, and affective processes.

In addition to providing clinically useful information about working with children, this book will also provide you with another type of information—information that will prove useful beyond working with children with anxious and phobic disorders. This book will introduce you to a broader perspective, a pragmatic "orientation," that we have found useful in organizing our thinking about all of the issues that we as mental health professionals face in our efforts to work with people in distress. Although we have found it useful in our work with children, this pragmatic orientation is not in itself an intervention approach. Nor is it a particular school of therapy in the way that we think of, for example, psychodynamic therapy, family therapy, cognitive behavior therapy, and so forth. You do *not*, as a consequence, have to be a "pragmatic therapist" to use the treatment we describe in this book. You *can be* a pragmatic therapist and use this treatment approach but, as you will see, you can also be psychodynamic, family, cognitive behavioral, etc.—or eclectic, integrative, or even atheoretical.

This pragmatic orientation is thus not a treatment approach in the usual sense. Rather, it is a way of thinking about clinical and research issues that goes beyond the particulars or specifics of any one treatment approach or school of therapy. This pragmatic orientation provides the broader perspective or framework that gives direction to all our intervention efforts. This pragmatic orientation has become the cornerstone of all of our efforts to develop effective interventions with children and adolescents. It helps to organize and guide the way we think about the clinical and research issues we face in implementing and evaluating our treatment approaches. Because it provides the framework that we use to organize our ideas about treatment, we will use this first chapter to introduce you to this pragmatic orientation.

THE PRAGMATIC TRADITION

"Pragmatic" is sometimes interpreted as meaning simple and expedient—and sometimes that's what pragmatic means. It can, however, mean more. Much more. The pragmatic tradition in modern thought, for example, has played a key role in shaping the way we think about many issues, including complex philosophical as well as theoretical and conceptual issues. The pragmatic principle is American in origin, and pragmatism encompasses a long and distinguished tradition that contains some of the most prominent thinkers in American philosophy, including Charles Pierce, William James, and John Dewey. Indeed, the pragmatic principle, the main contribution of pragmatism, has been proposed as American philosophy's most important contribution to 20th-century thinking (White, 1955). Moreover, pragmatism continues to have a strong influence on contemporary thought. In fact, in the works of the American philosopher Richard Rorty (see, e.g, Rorty, 1979, 1985, 1992), neopragmatism has emerged as one of the most prominent philosophical traditions in the world today—one that has been at the center of the revolutionary changes that have been taking place in contemporary philosophical thought. The concept of pragmatic that defines our orientation draws, in part, on this tradition. For us, pragmatic thus means something more than simply being expedient.

Pragmatic is sometimes also interpreted to mean atheoretical, eclectic, or even antitheoretical. Our pragmatic approach is none of these. As will become clear, we are not opposed to particular theories or schools of therapy that focus on particular processes, clinical procedures, or research methods. It is not even that we do not use theories to guide our work or that we do not think that theories are useful things to have. On the contrary, being pragmatic, we sometimes think that it is useful to focus on particular processes, procedures, and methods, just as we also think that theories are often useful things to have.

We are, however, opposed to the idea that any *one* particular theory provides the one right way to think about the clinical and research issues, or that any particular method or technique provides the *one* right way of working with children (or adults) in distress. Our pragmatic perspective, as a consequence, is not built on any basic assumptions about procedures/methods or grounded in any particular theoretical orientation. We do not, therefore, have foundational assumptions that dictate that one process or some processes (procedures, methods, etc.) are intrinsically more interesting, useful, or important than others.

If our pragmatic perspective is not defined by assumptions about the right way of thinking about any of these things, then what is it? One way to describe it is as *a way of thinking* about all of these things. A way of thinking about procedure and method. A way of thinking about theory and therapy, and about process and outcome. To borrow a phrase from James, it is an "attitude." It is an attitude of orientation toward *all* of human experience. This chapter will introduce you to the attitude or orientation that we call pragmatic—the attitude we bring to our work.

PRAGMATIC ATTITUDE

Being pragmatic means having an attitude, but not just any attitude. It means having an attitude with certain identifiable characteristics. We continue our description of what it means to be pragmatic by describing the characteristics of a pragmatic attitude, beginning with its problem-solving orientation.

Problem Solving

As we have already discussed, our pragmatic attitude does not begin with first principles or basic assumptions. Rather, where it begins is with concretely experienced human problems. It is an orientation that begins with concretely experienced human problems because the pragmatist adopts a *problem-solving* orientation.

Although there are many approaches to problem solving (see, e.g., Spivack, Platt, & Shure, 1976; Spivack & Shure, 1974, 1982), the pragmatist's approach is "pragmatic." As you might expect, we mean something specific by the concept of "pragmatic" problem solving. We mean more than simply being expedient in solving problems. Perhaps the most useful way of telling you what we mean by the concept of pragmatic problem solving is to first tell you what pragmatic problem solving is not. For example, one might be interested in problem solving as a domain of knowledge in the sense of "pure" knowledge. The pragmatist, however, is not interested in solving problems simply for the sake of solving problems or for the sake of developing "pure" knowledge. Quite the opposite, the pragmatist adopts a practical approach to problem solving and does not believe that solving problems can be separated from the practical effects or consequences of solving problems. To borrow (and paraphrase) another expression from James, the practical meaning and significance of any problem can always be brought down to some particular consequence, in our future practical experience, whether active or passive. For the pragmatist, this "pragmatic" orientation provides a practical test of the significance of a problem. If the outcome or consequence of solving a particular problem will have no effect on the quality of life of real human beings, then solving the problem has no practical significance.

For example, debate in the clinical and research literatures (and at times in our own center) comes to focus on abstract or general theoretical and methodological issues that have to do with questions such as which theoretical orientation provides the best clinical or research framework, what are the best clinical procedures or research methods, etc. For the pragmatist, the results of the application of the practical test of significance to such general questions are clear. The pragmatist does not consider it particularly useful to resolve such general questions or to expend time and resources in attempting to solve such "problems," because knowing whether cognitive is in some abstract or general way better than behavioral (or psychodynamic, family, etc.) does not solve the problem of identifying the most efficacious technique or procedure to use with a specific population and problem in a particular context. The pragmatist, in other words, does not consider it particularly useful to resolve such general questions (even if it were possible to do so) because the outcome or consequence of the effort will contribute little to increasing the effectiveness of the particular therapeutic procedures we use with specific populations and problems. The type of question the pragmatic therapist would prefer to ask (and attempt to answer) is whether a specific technique of cognitive therapy, such as the correction of patients' faulty cognition, is better than a specific technique of psychodynamic therapy, such as the interpretation of patients' words or actions, in the treatment of a specific childhood phobia. The pragmatic therapist, in other words, is interested in doing what is useful and what works with particular problems and populations.

Saying that the pragmatist is not interested in developing "pure" knowledge, however, is not the same thing as saying that the pragmatist is opposed to knowledge development. Quite the opposite. As we have already pointed out, we have at our center ongoing programs of research that focus on knowledge development. Our orientation toward knowledge development, however, focuses on "practical" knowledge. The pragmatist thinks that the solution to problems cannot be separated from the practical effects or consequences of the solutions on particular human beings in specific contexts, because what is a successful solution in one context may be a more or less successful solution in another context. The pragmatist thus also considers knowledge to be contextual in significance. Which brings us to the second characteristic of our pragmatic attitude, namely, that it is *contextualistic*. We have discussed what we mean when we say that a pragmatic attitude includes a problem-solving orientation. Now we need to say some things about what it means to be contextualistic.

Contextualistic

Our pragmatic attitude provides an alternative perspective on the meaning and significance of the concepts and constructs that are used in working with children (or adults) in distress. Traditionally, concepts and constructs (reinforcement and contingency, unconscious and instinctual, schema and script, etc.) are associated with particular theories and approaches (behavioral, psychodynamic, cognitive, etc.). In this frame, concepts and constructs derive their meaning and significance from the theoretical frameworks in which they are embedded. We, on the other hand, do not believe that concepts derive their meaning and significance from the theoretical frameworks or approaches in which they are embedded; we believe they derive their meaning and significance from the "contexts" in which they are *used*. Indeed, although we consider theories useful things to have, we consider the utility of theories themselves to be contextual. That is, we consider concepts of all types and at all levels (e.g., theoretical constructs, clinical procedures, research methods) to be contextual in significance.

If the pragmatist considers even theories to be contextual in significance, does this mean that the pragmatist is "relativistic"? Does this mean that pragmatism is simply another example of relativism? We think not. Relativism is a term that is commonly used to describe the view that every belief is as good as every other (Rorty, 1985). Although the pragmatist views knowledge as contingent and contextual, the pragmatist does not view every belief as being as good as every other. Nor does the pragmatist think that nothing can be evaluated true or false, better or worse, or right or wrong. On the contrary, the pragmatist's recognition of the contingent and contextual nature of knowledge also results in a recognition that knowledge is *particularlistic* and in every case necessarily rooted in the reality of specific problems in specific contexts. For specific problems in specific contexts, existing hierarchies of assumptions and beliefs about the world can be (and are) used to solve problems. Moreover, from the pragmatist's point of view, there is no good reason for not accepting, at least provisionally, existing knowledge and beliefs about the world in solving problems.

Existing knowledge and beliefs about the world, however, are not final. Existing hierarchies of beliefs do not define the end point of human knowledge; rather, they constitute the starting point. For the pragmatist, the validity of existing beliefs about the world can (and should) be evaluated with regard to their success in contributing to the successful solution to concretely experienced problems. And as conditions change, existing beliefs can (and should) be evaluated with regard to their success in contributing to the solution to new problems.

Successful problem solving, however, involves more than passively responding to changing conditions.

In proposing his view of knowledge as contextual in significance, Dewey (1922) proposed that successful problem solving has the potential for enlarging and enriching human horizons. Human goal-oriented behavior involves both means and ends. *Ends* refers to goals, aims, outcomes, etc.; *means* refers to the plans, procedures, methods, strategies, etc., by which goals, aims, or outcomes are achieved or accomplished. Ends, however, are not fixed categories toward which we aspire; nor are the means by which they are achieved fixed. Means and ends are concepts pertinent to particular problems and find their validity in their success in contributing to the solution to these problems. Ends direct means, but ends themselves can become means. Ends that have been successfully achieved become the means to achieve ends that formerly may have been not only unattainable but even unimaginable. Consequently, the successful solution to concretely experienced practical problems has the effect of expanding the boundaries of horizons.

The pragmatist, consequently, is *not* relativistic. In fact, the pragmatist objects to the concept that every belief is as good as every other. The pragmatist objects to the concept that every belief is as good as every other because the pragmatist thinks that as things change they can (and do) change for the better. That is, the pragmatist thinks that things change and that they can change for the worse, but that they can also change for the better. One way that things can change for the better is that as they change, human beings can understand how and why things change, and human beings can (and do) come up with better ideas and ways of doing things. The pragmatist objects to relativism because he or she believes that it is possible to come up with new and better ideas and ways of doing things.

Thus, in addition to adopting a problem-solving orientation, we also adopt a view of concepts and constructs as contextual in significance. Moreover, we mean something specific by the concept of "contextual in significance." We mean that we consider the utility and validity of concepts to be pertinent to particular problems, and that the utility and validity of concepts are to be found in their success in contributing to the solution to these problems.

WHAT DOES IT MEAN TO BE A PRAGMATIC THERAPIST?

Now that we have provided you with a broad overview and introduction to what we mean by a pragmatic attitude, it will be helpful if we begin to introduce you to some of the implications that such a perspective has for you as a mental health professional who works with children. What, in other words, does it mean to be a pragmatic therapist?

Although the book as a whole is devoted to answering this question in detail, the basic answer to this question is relatively simple. It is a two-part answer. First, what it means to be a pragmatic therapist in the most general sense is defined by the attitude we bring to the treatment process. A pragmatic therapist is someone who adopts an attitude toward the process of therapy that is problem solving and contextualistic (and all that that implies). This means that if your attitude toward therapy shares some (or all) of the features implied by these characteristics, then, to that extent you are already a pragmatic therapist. Regardless of the therapeutic tradition with which you identify, to the extent that you are willing to draw on other traditions (orientations, approaches, procedures, methods, etc.) to work with particular populations and problems in specific contexts, you are a pragmatic therapist.

The second part of what it means to be a pragmatic therapist has to do with what pragmatic therapists do. But what do pragmatic therapists do? At this point, if you are beginning to get a feel for what it means to be pragmatic, you will recognize that this is the type of question that a pragmatist would rather avoid than answer—abstract, general, and nonspecific. You will appreciate that from a pragmatic perspective, this is a type of question that really has no answer—or, more precisely, that has no determinate answer. This question does not have a determinate answer because there are as many answers to this question as there are populations, problems, and contexts in which the pragmatic therapist does therapy. *A pragmatic therapist does what is useful and what works*. A pragmatic therapist does what is useful and what works, and the largest part of this book will be devoted to telling you what we as pragmatic therapists do with children with anxiety and phobic disorders.

Thus, although we have used a variety of words in a variety of ways in describing our orientation, in the end it really is relatively simple. It boils down to an attitude—an "attitude of orientation"—that includes a practical problem-solving orientation that focuses on concretely experienced problems in specific contexts. Although relatively simple, such a perspective does involve a reorientation in the ways that many of us are used to thinking about human behavior and development. We have provided you with a brief introduction to some of the broader implications of such an orientation, and we will touch on these issues throughout the book.

The pragmatic attitude that we bring to our work with children and adolescents did not develop suddenly or spontaneously. Rather, this attitude is grounded in many years of clinical and research experience involving a variety of theoretical orientations, clinical procedures, and research methods. Our own personal professional experiences, for example, include extensive work in the area of cognitive behavioral assessment and intervention (e.g., Silverman & Kurtines, 1996) and in family therapy assessment and intervention (e.g., Kurtines & Szapocznik, 1996). In the process, we have learned a great deal from these troubled youth and their families.

This book is about how you can help children troubled by anxiety and distress that disrupt their lives and the lives of the members of their families. We said, however, that this book is also about an orientation that we have found extremely useful in organizing our ideas and our ways of thinking about how to help these children. Thus, this book will introduce you to an orientation or perspective that has broad potential for helping you in all of your work in treating people in distress. Now that we have described some of the more general implications of this perspective, we can turn to how we have applied this perspective to helping children experiencing distress related to anxiety and phobic disorders.

Evaluation

In turning to how we have applied our pragmatic orientation to helping children in distress, we begin with evaluation. Our goal is to share with you some of the ideas and ways of doing things that we have found useful for assessing phobic and anxiety disorders in children. In the process, we also illustrate how the "attitude of orientation" that makes us pragmatic—the problem-solving and contextualistic orientation—has been useful in our evaluation work.

For the pragmatist, we noted, human goal-oriented behavior involves both means and ends. *Ends* refers to goals, aims, outcomes, etc., and *means* refers to the plans, procedures, methods, strategies, etc., by which goals, aims, or outcomes are achieved or accomplished. In this case, our end or goal is to identify the type of help that children need, and evaluation is the means for accomplishing this goal. Our problem, then, is identifying the *most useful* means for evaluating the type of help that children need.

Part II is comprised of two chapters. Chapter 2, Assessment, focuses on the most useful means for evaluating the childhood problems that we are interested in in this book, namely, problems with excessive fear and anxiety. Chapter 2 thus illustrates the types of methods that can be used to evaluate these problems and the contexts in which these methods can be applied. Chapter 3, Assessment for Diagnosis, focuses more specifically on assessment for diagnosis because of the central role that diagnosis has come to play in the mental health field.

2

Assessment

Courses and books on assessment often focus on methods and techniques, such as the technical aspects of administration, scoring, and interpretation of psychological tests. However, our focus in this chapter is not on technical issues. Rather, our focus is on the ideas and ways of doing things that we have found useful in the work we have done on assessing children with phobic and anxiety disorders. Although we recognize that it is important to have a solid background in the technical issues related to assessment methods, we also consider it just as important to have a "pragmatic," problem-focused orientation that recognizes a full range of goals as well as means. The goal of our assessment activities is, after all, more than solving technical and methodological problems; our ultimate goal is to identify the type of help that children in distress need.

ASSESSMENT GOALS

Mental health professionals are frequently called upon to evaluate children in contexts that are complex as well as diverse. In contexts of complexity and uncertainty there are a number of ways that might be used to minimize the difficulty of making decisions about assessment. One way, for example, is to fall into a pattern of routinely relying on a particular assessment method. Relying on a particular assessment method—perhaps the one with which we have become most familiar or the one that is most consistent with our theoretical approach—provides a solution to the problem of choosing an assessment method; it becomes the assessment method of choice by default. Moreover, it is a strategy that may work well in many or most of the contexts in which we need to make decisions about assessment.

The pragmatic attitude that we tend to use in making our choices of assessment methods, however, serves to remind us not to let our assumptions about assessment get in the way of choosing and using the most effective methods. Like everyone else, we have our preferred methods—methods that we have successfully used in the past (indeed, some that we have even developed), and we too frequently fall back on these methods. (And we sometimes have passionate discussions over the relative merits of these methods.) In the end, however, the criterion we advocate, and try to put into practice in making our assessment decisions, is *what works with the particular problem we are trying to solve*. We fall back on "what works" as the criterion because it helps us to accomplish our ultimate goal—namely, to help the children and families with whom we work.

Our pragmatic orientation, however, helps by keeping us focused on particular problems in *specific contexts*. In the case of making decisions about assessment methods, for example, it directs us to begin by asking what will be the assessment setting. For example, will the assessment take place in a private practice? A school setting? An outpatient clinic? Although relatively simple, we begin with context because some assessment methods are more usable or feasible than others in particular settings.

A second and sometimes more challenging task is identifying the *specific goal* that the assessment method will help us to accomplish. Indeed, deciding on which assessment method to use in any one of these settings without knowing the eventual goal is problematic—sort of like going on a trip with no ultimate destination or purpose. Such a trip leads nowhere and accomplishes nothing except to waste time, money, and effort. Not knowing in advance what our assessment goal is also makes it more likely that we will use inappropriate methods of assessment. This is because particular assessment goals are better reached through the use of particular assessment methods than through the use of others.

A third and sometimes the most challenging task is choosing the "best" assessment method that will help us to accomplish the specific goal in that particular setting. For the pragmatist, to say that something is best is the same thing as saying that it is good, right, desirable, useful, and so on. Such normative concepts derive their meaning and significance from the context in which they are used. Thus, for each setting or context in which we have to make a decision about assessment, we ask what problem the assessment method will help us to solve or what issue it will resolve. We then choose the assessment method that helps us to accomplish the goal of solving this problem. For example, in each of the assessment settings we describe below, there is a need to conduct some type of assessment to solve a problem, answer a question, clarify an issue, or accomplish a goal. Because choosing the "best" method for use in a particular setting is so central to the assessment process, we will devote a large part of this chapter to discussing this issue.

Finally, our problem-solving orientation is helpful in that most difficult of all contexts, namely, when we do not know what to do next. Choosing assessment methods is sometimes simple and straightforward, and sometimes it is not. When it is not, it helps to have an orientation that organizes our thinking. As noted, however, when it comes to solving complex or difficult problems, having an orientation is not a substitute for a good working knowledge of available methods of assessment, including the most common goals of assessment such as screening, diagnosing, quantifying symptoms, and so on. But an orientation helps to provide guidelines for our problem-solving activities when new contexts, new populations, or new issues arise that are out of the ordinary, at least with respect to our own personal or professional experiences.

What we have done so far is introduce you to the type of pragmatic attitude that we adopt when faced with choosing assessment methods. Up to this point, the introduction has been pretty abstract (we are, after all, talking about an "attitude"). We now illustrate these points more concretely by describing below several assessment settings, each of which involves a problem you will most likely be asked to solve at some point in your work with children with phobic and anxiety disorders. In fact, some or all of these situations may sound like *déjà vu* to you, as each one occurs rather commonly in clinical practice. We ask that you envision yourself in each.

ASSESSMENT SETTINGS

1 | A local school district is planning to develop an "anxiety management" program for children who are anxiety-prone and who experience difficulties with excessive anxiety. You have been called in by the local school district as a consultant. Specifically, the school district has asked for your help in deciding which children to include in the program.

2 | You are the director of a busy child outpatient clinic. For some time now, you have been feeling that each staff member's own idiosyncratic clinical interview is resulting in many inaccurate diagnoses. You would like to improve the clinic's diagnostic procedures, including the diagnosis of comorbid conditions. You are particularly interested in improving diagnoses of childhood anxiety and phobic disorders, as you are interested in developing a specialty clinic for these types of problems.

3 | With many of your child inpatients, you frequently notice many problematic symptoms and behaviors that relate to anxiety and its disorders. If left unattended, they frequently interfere with the children's treatment. You would like to be able to identify and quantify problematic anxious symptoms and behaviors early on and then target them for treatment, if necessary.

4 | In the current competitive environment of managed care/health service delivery, you and your associates in your group practice for children and families are feeling that your group needs to move toward documenting that your treatments with your patients "work." Specifically, you want to initiate a method of gauging your patients' progress at the end of treatment. You wish to do this with all of your patients, particularly those who are treated for problems with excessive fear and anxiety.

5 | Although you usually learn a great deal from talking to your anxious child patients and their parents, you are also struck by how difficult it is for so many of them to inform you about the subtleties of many of the child's problematic behaviors. Not only is it difficult for them to detail "what the child looks like when he or she becomes anxious," it is also difficult for them to specify the situations or objects that elicit anxiety. You are interested in broadening your current methods of assessment in your practice so that this type of information is also obtained.

At first glance, this array of situations appears to represent a diverse and discrete matrix of settings with no common theme. You may have had previous experience with some of these types of settings but not others. If the situation in which you find yourself is one in which you have had no experience, you may feel that some decision-making guidelines would help. This is where our pragmatic orientation can be of use.

Our pragmatic attitude dictates that we suspend judgment with respect to what will work and what will not. We do not want to simply "fall back" on our favorite assessment method, whatever it happens to be. It may be our eventual choice (and it may work fine), but it is not a good idea to resort to it without considering the available alternatives. In addition to providing some guidelines about what *not to do*, our pragmatic perspective also provides some guidelines about what *to do*.

The concept of context dictates that in deciding on what assessment method to use, we first identify the setting and the goal. For our purposes, by "setting" we mean the specific situation wherein the assessment takes place (e.g., private practice, clinic, school). By "goal" we mean the purpose or function of the assessment (e.g., the "question" that you are seeking to answer or are being asked to answer).

The concept of pragmatic dictates that in deciding on what assessment method to use, we choose the method that is "most useful" in a particular setting. Part of what it means to be useful is that the method is clinically feasible in a particular setting. More importantly, it also means choosing the method that

Table 2.1. Illustration of Settings, Goals,[a] and Assessment Methods

Setting	Goal	Method
School	Screening	Self-rating scale
Outpatient clinic	Differential diagnosis	Structured interview
Inpatient clinic	Identifying and quantifying anxious symptoms	Self-rating scale
Group practice	Treatment outcome	Structured interview or self-rating scale
Private practice	Obtaining more detailed information	Daily diary and behavioral exposure task

[a]These goals are not unique to these particular types of settings, but they are linked here as a way to illustrate our approach toward assessment.

ultimately works best in accomplishing the goal of identifying the needs of children whom we wish to help. As we discuss in more detail later, what works best means choosing methods that have at least some scientific evidence of utility—i.e., reliability and validity.

In the first situation, for example, the school district has a very specific goal in mind: how to identify which children should be included in a program because they may be at risk for anxiety. Because the contextualistic part of our orientation directs that we focus on the goals in this particular setting, we draw on our knowledge of assessment to translate the question into one of the common assessment goals. In this case, the assessment goal that matches the question is *screening*. In the second situation, in which you are the director of a busy child outpatient clinic, the question is how to improve the accuracy of the diagnoses assigned by your clinic's staff. In this case, the assessment goal is *differential diagnosis*. In the third situation, in which you work in a child inpatient clinic, the goal is to learn about children's anxiety symptoms and problematic behaviors ahead of time, so that they do not "catch you by surprise" and interfere with the children's treatment. So here the goal of assessment is *identifying and quantifying* problematic anxious symptoms or behaviors. Fourth is the situation in which your group practice is faced with a very basic problem—how can you get some sense as to whether or not your treatments "work?" In this case, the goal of assessment is to gauge *treatment outcome*. In the final situation you wish to go beyond your patients' self-reports. Here the goal is to *obtain more detailed information* about your patients' problem behaviors. These settings and goals are summarized in Table 2.1.

ASSESSMENT METHODS

Now that we have identified the goal for each of the assessment settings, we discuss some of the concrete issues and details involved in identifying the assessment method that is best to use in that setting and for that goal. As we have noted, within our pragmatic framework, the concept of "best" means the same thing as most useful, and what is most useful is contextual in significance; that is, "most useful" is a concept to be evaluated in relation to a particular problem and the actual (and foreseeable) alternatives for solving that problem. Choosing the best or most useful assessment method thus depends on our being able to effectively identify the goal, our having a solid background in all the available methods of assessment (including an understanding of the advantages and disadvantages of each method), and our being pragmatic in our efforts to solve the problem.

Screening

In the first situation, you need to recommend to the local school district a method that it can use for screening children who are anxiety-prone and should thus be included in an anxiety management program. In essence you are being asked to help the school district differentiate a group of symptomatic children from those who are asymptomatic. In choosing a method that can be used for such differentiation, our orientation, as we have noted, dictates that we focus on both the setting (i.e., the school) and the goal (i.e., screening).

First let's consider the characteristics of the school setting. As we all know, most school settings do not have the luxury of expending a great deal of staff, time, or funds on tasks that are nonacademic. Hence, we need to choose a method that is low-cost and that requires minimal time and effort on the part of the staff and the students.

Typically, once we have identified the setting and the characteristics of the setting we can quickly move on and focus on the goal. This is not the case in the school setting just described, however. If our knowledge about the various methods of assessment is solid, we realize that the number of feasible methods for use in this setting is limited; and one method already stands out from the rest. Specifically, we know that child self-rating scales are clearly the most feasible because no other assessment method costs so little and is so easy to administer and to score. We also know that rating scales, because of their objective scoring procedure, minimize the role of clinical inference and interpretation; so there is no need to use highly trained staff for administration/scoring. In addition, the self-rating scales for childhood anxiety clearly contain questions that would be of concern to the members of the school district; that is, the scales possess "face validity."

Several child self-rating scales have been developed for assessing anxiety in children and may be used for screening. Table 2.2 presents a brief descriptive summary of these measures. The most widely used measures assess global or

Table 2.2. Self-Rating Scales for Screening

Scale	Description	Psychometrics
Revised Children's Manifest Anxiety Scale (RCMAS; Reynolds & Richmond, 1978, 1985)	37 items; yields a total anxiety score and three factor scale scores (Physiological Anxiety, Worry/Oversensitivity, and Social Concerns/Concentration) and a Lie Scale score	*Internal consistency:* Alpha coefficients were greater than .80 for the total scale score; alpha coefficients for each factor scale range from .64 to .76 *Reliability:* Test–retest coefficients of .98 and .94 for the total scale score and Lie scale score using a 3-week interval; .68 and .58 using a 9-month interval *Validity:* Positive and significant correlations between RCMAS total scores and other anxiety/fear measures. Findings more mixed when multitrait multimethod methodology is used.
State-Trait Anxiety Inventory for Children (STAIC; Spielberger, 1973)	Two 20-item scales—the A-Trait Scale and the A-State Scale. The A-Trait scale designed to measure chronic cross-situational anxiousness. The A-State scale designed to measure acute, transitory anxiousness	*Internal consistency:* Alpha coefficients range from .80 to .90 for A-State and approximately .80 for A-Trait scale *Reliability:* Test–retest coefficients range from .65 to .72 for A-State, .44 to .94 for A-Trait *Validity:* Positive and significant correlations between STAIC scores and other anxiety/fear measures. Findings more mixed when multitrait multimethod methodology is used.
Social Anxiety Scale for Children Revised, (SASC-R; La Greca & Stone, 1993)	22 items; yields a total score and three factor scale scores [Fear of Negative Evaluation (FNE), Social Avoidance and Distress in New Situations (SAD-New), and General Social Avoidance and Distress (SAD-G)]	*Internal consistency:* Alpha coefficients for each of the SASC-R subscales reflected acceptable internal consistency with all coefficients greater than .65 *Reliability:* Standardized reliability coefficients were .86, .78, and .69 for the FNE, SAD-New, and SAD-G scales, respectively *Validity:* Confirmatory factor analysis revealed a good fit for the three-factor model. Also, discriminant validity supported in that neglected and rejected children reported more social anxiety than accepted children

(continued)

Table 2.2. Continued

Scale	Description	Psychometrics
Social Phobia Anxiety Inventory for Children (SPAIC; Beidel, Turner, & Morris, 1995)	26 items; yields a total anxiety/distress score and three factor scale scores (Assertiveness/General Conversation, Traditional Social Encounters, and Public Performance)	*Internal consistency:* Alpha coefficient for the total scale score was .95 *Reliability:* Test–retest coefficient was .86 using a 2-week interval, .63 using a 9-month interval *Validity:* Positive and significant correlations between the SPAIC scores and other self-report anxiety/fear measures, with a range of .41 to .53
Test Anxiety Scale for Children (TASC; Sarason et al., 1958)	30 items designed to measure children's anxiety in test-taking situations	*Internal consistency:* Alpha coefficients ranged from .82 to .90 *Reliability:* Test–retest coefficients ranged from .44 to .85 *Validity:* Positive and significant correlation with teachers' ratings from .09 to .31 for different grades
Child Anxiety Sensitivity Index (CASI; Silverman et al., 1991)	18-item scale designed to measure how aversive child views anxious symptoms	*Internal consistency:* Alpha coefficient of .87 *Reliability:* Test–retest coefficients range from .62 to .78 using a 1–2-week interval *Validity:* Explained variance in the prediction of trait anxiety unaccounted for by other anxiety/fear measures
Fear Survey Schedule for Children–Revised (FSSC-R; Ollendick, 1983)	80 items; yields a total fear score and five factor scale scores (Fear of Failure and Criticism, Fear of the Unknown, Fear of Injury and Small Animals, Fear of Danger and Death, Medical Fears)	*Internal consistency:* Alpha coefficients range from .92 to .95 *Reliability:* Test–retest coefficients were .82 using a 1-week interval and .55 using a 3-month interval *Validity:* Positive and significant coefficients between FSSC-R total scores and other anxiety measures approximately .50

diffuse levels of anxiety. These are the Revised Children's Manifest Anxiety Scale (Reynolds & Richmond, 1978) and the State Trait Anxiety Inventory for Children (Spielberger, 1973). Questionnaires have also been developed that assess levels of social anxiety in children (the Social Anxiety Scale for Children–Revised [La Greca & Stone, 1993] and the Social Phobia Anxiety Inventory for Children [Beidel, Turner, & Morris, 1996], as well as other specific types of anxiety, such as anxiety about school events (particularly, tests) (the Test Anxiety Scale for Children [Sarason, Davidson, Lighthall, & Waite, 1958]) and anxiety about experiencing physiological anxious symptomatology (the Child Anxiety Sensitivity Index [Silverman, Fleisig, Rabian, & Peterson, 1991]). If you are interested in assessing the related construct of fear, you might find the Fear Survey Schedule for Children–Revised (FSSC-R; Ollendick, 1983) to be most useful. In particular, you are likely to find that children with different types of anxiety disorders would endorse different and specific types of fears (although the total FSSC-R scores themselves would not be able to differentiate among the children) (Last, Francis, & Strauss, 1989). For example, children with Separation Anxiety Disorder would likely endorse fears about separation, such as "getting lost"; children with Generalized Anxiety Disorder would likely endorse social and performance fears, such as "being teased."

Now that we have identified child self-rating scales as being most feasible for use in the school setting and have listed the most commonly used measures, let's focus our attention on the specific goal of screening. Based on the scientific evidence, just how useful are these child self-rating scales for screening for childhood anxiety? First, on the negative side, we know that in an attempt to present themselves in a positive light to adult testers, children may respond to the demand characteristics of the assessment situation by responding in socially desirable ways on these measures (La Greca, 1990). Steps can be taken, however, to limit the potential problem of children presenting themselves in a positive light or in a socially desirable way. Most important of these is the use of carefully worded instructions (usually a part of the questionnaires) such as "all children have different feelings"; "we are interested in how you feel about things"; and "there are no right or wrong answers."

Assuming that appropriate steps have been taken to reduce the potential of child social desirability, are the child self-rating scales useful for screening? On the positive side, we know that they are more useful than parent- or teacher-rating scales. In particular, there is now general consensus that it is more useful to elicit information from parents and teachers about observable, or objective, child behaviors (Loeber, Green, & Lahey, 1990). It is more useful, on the other hand, to elicit information from the children themselves about subjective child behaviors, such as anxiety. This belief is based on findings that children report fewer conduct problems but more anxiety and affective symptoms than do their parents during diagnostic interviewing procedures (e.g., Herjanic, Herjanic, Brown, & Wheatt, 1975).

Although the child self-rating scales are more useful than parent- or teacher-rating scales, are they useful in and of themselves? To adequately consider this issue, it is important to understand the concepts of sensitivity and specificity. Sensitivity is the percentage of individuals who receive the diagnosis who are positively identified by the rating scale (true positives); specificity is the percentage of individuals who do not receive the diagnosis and who are not identified by the rating scale as anxious (true negatives) (Vecchio, 1966). In terms of screening for anxiety disorders in children, the available child self-rating scales are likely to select more false positives than true positives (Costello & Angold, 1988). In other words, children identified as anxious at an initial screen are likely not to be so identified the next time. For example, using the RCMAS with outpatient boys (ages 8 to 12), Mattison, Bagnato, and Brubaker (1988) found the sensitivity rates to be 41%, 36%, and 48%, depending on the cutoff technique employed. Hodges (1990) found the STAIC to have a sensitivity of 42% and a specificity of 79% in a sample of inpatient children (ages 6 to 13).

In addition to sensitivity and specificity, however, there is also the more general issue as to whether these self-rating scales are measuring what they were designed to measure, namely, the construct of anxiety. A large number of studies (both monomethod and multimethod) have found large correlations between self-rating scales of anxiety and depression such that no meaningful discrimination between self-reported anxiety and depression could be identified (e.g., Norvell, Brophy, & Finch, 1985; Saylor, Finch, Spirito, & Bennett, 1984; Treiber & Mabe, 1987). This has led to the suggestion that a general negative affectivity component is common to both anxiety and depression disorders and measures in child (e.g., Finch, Lipovsky, & Casat, 1989; King, Ollendick, & Gullone, 1991) and adult populations (e.g., Watson and Clark, 1984). However, although negative affectivity appears to be a common underlying feature, investigators have also found that one factor that appears to distinguish between anxiety and depression in both children and adults is positive affectivity (e.g., Lonigan, Carey, & Finch, 1994; Watson, Clark, & Carey, 1988). That is, negative affectivity appears to be related to both anxiety and depression; low positive affectivity appears to be related only to depression. Accordingly, a possible way to improve the distinctiveness of anxiety and depression self-rating scales is to assess the degree to which respondents report high positive affective states and then to infer depression from the relative absence of such experiences. In other words, a greater number of items contained in self-rating scales need to be reflective of positive affectivity—not negative affectivity (Watson & Kendall, 1989).

Taken altogether, at present there is no single method of assessment that can perfectly screen for anxiety disorders in children. The situation has been summarized well by Costello and Angold (1988): "If it were really possible to identify all true cases and true noncases using a brief self-report questionnaire, large areas of diagnostic psychiatry would be redundant. It is unrealistic to expect this level of accuracy…. Perhaps the term 'screen' is unhelpful…; the process is more like trawling through a population with a net; one will catch some of the fish one wants, miss others, and pick up all sorts of other species that will have to be selected out later" (pp. 729–730).

In light of this, perhaps the "best" way to screen for childhood anxiety is to employ a two-stage process. At the first stage, a self-rating scale is administered to the children. Departures from the "norm" are then determined based on standard deviation units that define a particular percentile of the sample. Children who are found to depart from the norm in this way are thereby identified as having to undergo more precise and comprehensive assessments at the next stage, using the method that is discussed in the next section.

Diagnosing

In the second situation, you direct a busy child outpatient clinic. (Or, perhaps just in your own practice, you would like to feel more confident about the diagnoses of your patients' problems.) In such situations your goal is to improve your diagnostic procedures, including the diagnosis of comorbid conditions. In choosing a method that can be used for diagnosis, our orientation, once again, dictates that we focus on both the setting and the goal. In the case of the child outpatient clinic, our pragmatic problem solving guides us to select a method that can be administered in a reasonable amount of time to the many children who pass through this busy clinic and that can be readily learned by the clinic's staff.

Although our focus on the setting has helped us to begin to organize our ideas about the types of assessment methods to select, we realize that, unlike in the school setting, in the child outpatient setting there are several methods that could be used. Consequently, we turn our attention to the goal. This should help us to further organize our ideas. In this example your goal is diagnosis, i.e., to more accurately classify problematic child behaviors ("diagnose") into the various categories that make up the DSM classification scheme, particularly those categories that make up the anxiety and phobic disorders.

In light of this goal, based on the scientific evidence, which assessment method is "best" to use for diagnosing? Of all available methods of assessment, the interview is the best to use for diagnosis. The interview, in addition to providing primary diagnoses, such as those of anxiety disorders, provides diagnoses of comorbid disorders. Because there is a great deal to be said about using interviews for assessing for diagnosis, we devote the next chapter entirely to this assessment goal.

Identifying Anxiety Symptoms and Behaviors

In the next example, in which you work in a child inpatient clinic, your goal is to identify anxiety symptoms and behaviors early on in the patients, so that they do not catch you by surprise and interfere with the children's treatment. There are generally two best methods of identifying problematic child anxiety symptoms and behaviors. Both methods are feasible to use in this setting. One method is the use of one of the child anxiety self-rating scales, discussed earlier under Screening. Specifically, you can administer one (or more) of the scales to the child and examine the specific items that have been endorsed. These items may then be selected as subsequent targets for treatment.

In addition to identifying anxiety symptoms and behaviors, you may also be interested in quantifying these symptoms and behaviors. This may be useful to you because you might want to know, albeit tentatively, the extent to which these symptoms and behaviors represent a particular problem area for the child. Indeed, the ratings scales were specifically designed for this purpose. One standard deviation from the normative mean has often been taken as an index of some type of clinically significant problem. But recall what was said earlier when we talked about using child self-rating scales for screening: namely, that groups that are defined in this way are not necessarily defined as "anxious" via diagnoses—studies comparing diagnoses with presentation on various rating scales demonstrate that optimal cutoff scores that maximize classification accuracy have a high rate of false positives and false negatives. (Also recall the other limitations of these scales, such as the potential of social desirability, etc.) Nevertheless, obtaining a quantitative index can be useful in that it may assist you in determining whether further assessment of anxiety symptoms and behaviors is warranted.

Another way to identify and quantify problematic child anxious symptoms and behaviors is to use particular subsections of a child- or parent-structured interview schedule as minimodules. For example, if you are interested in learning whether a child is experiencing difficulties with the symptoms of Generalized Anxiety Disorder, you could ask the interview questions contained on any of the schedules that cover this diagnostic subcategory. The particular items that the child (or parent) endorses on the interview would then represent the symptoms or behaviors that are most problematic for or relevant to him or her. You can also quantify the number of symptoms reported, and determine whether or not diagnostic criteria have been met. Using interview schedules to identify and quantify problematic child anxious symptoms and behaviors offers the advantage of asking questions that are clearly in line with DSM criteria—something that the available child self-rating scales do not do. Like the rating scales, however, demand characteristics of the interview have the potential of pulling socially desirable responses from children. Carefully worded instructions may also once again be needed to help minimize this potential.

Gauging Treatment Outcome

In the fourth situation, in which you are part of a group practice, you are interested in obtaining some estimate as to whether or not the treatments your group delivers "work." You are particularly interested in doing this for your anxious and fearful child patients' treatments. Thus, your goal is to gauge your patients' treatment outcome.

We should note at the onset that assessing treatment outcome is a complex and difficult goal. To fully and adequately assess treatment outcome, it is necessary to conduct controlled group research studies or single case studies. This type of work usually occurs in clinical research settings in which many critical factors can be controlled (e.g., specific patient characteristics, experience of therapists, etc.). It is usually not feasible to attend to such issues in clinical settings. Nevertheless, some gauging of treatment outcome is still possible. In our view, this can be done by using a child-structured interview schedule (with both child and parent versions being administered), and at least one child self-rating scale. These should be administered both before treatment and at the end of treatment. Specifically, using one of the interview schedules (discussed in the next chapter), you can determine whether or not the child continues to meet diagnostic criteria. Ratings of severity and interference, which are contained on many of the interview schedules, should also be obtained pre- and posttreatment. This will allow you to gauge whether the degree of impairment caused by the anxiety or phobia problems has been reduced. Also worthwhile is to examine whether the number of behaviors or symptoms endorsed by the child and parent on the interview schedules' various symptoms scales have been reduced posttreatment.

If it is not feasible to administer the entire interview schedule over again, you can just readminister the sections of the schedule that cover the specific anxiety or phobia problems that were targeted for treatment. For example, if treatment focused on improving a child's distress in social evaluative situations, then the questions that pertain to Social Phobia would be the ones asked. Thus, in just a few minutes and by asking just a few questions, you can gauge whether some treatment gains have been made. The results of this questioning may also be shared with the child and parent to help them recognize the progress that has been made.

In terms of using the child self-rating scales, the particular ones we would recommend using would depend on the specific nature of the child's problem(s). As noted earlier, for example, the Fear Survey Schedule for Children–Revised (Ollendick, 1983) might be used when working with a child with multiple fears; the Children's Manifest Anxiety Scale–Revised (Reynolds & Richmond, 1978) might be used when working with a child with more general, diffuse anxiety problems; the Social Anxiety Scale for Children–Revised (La Greca & Stone, 1993) when working with a child with social anxiety problems; or the Childhood Anxiety Sensitivity Index (Silverman et al., 1991) when working with a child with panic attacks. As mentioned before, these self-rating scales are generally useful for identifying particular symptoms of anxiety as well as for quantifying levels of anxiety or fear. In this regard, they can serve as an efficient, though rough, gauge of treatment progress (e.g., did scores decline?).

Nevertheless, the use of the above methods to gauge treatment outcome needs to be done cautiously. Declines have been found to occur with these scores, irrespective of treatment (e.g., Edelbrock, Costello, Dulcan, Conover, & Kalàs, 1985; Finch, Saylor, Edwards, & McIntosh, 1987; Nelson & Politano, 1990; Silverman & Eisen, 1992). Consequently, it is recommended that when you use them to gauge outcome, they should be administered at least two times prior to the actual treatment—once at the very initial screening or assessment, and again immediately prior to treatment (Finch et al., 1987). This will help in determining whether the observed declines are due to treatment itself or to factors that have nothing to do with treatment.

In summary, in the absence of systematic treatment outcome evaluation—either through systematic group research designs or through single case study designs—any "conclusion" drawn about treatment outcome needs to be viewed as tentative and merely suggestive. Despite this, we are of the view that therapists need not do "all or nothing at all." We believe that even an estimate, no matter how rough, is better than nothing at all. At least one can determine, after conducting a certain type of treatment with a reasonable number of cases, whether some positive change is occurring or patients seem to be getting worse.

Obtaining a Richer Picture of Problem Behaviors

In the final situation, your goal is to obtain more detailed information about your anxious patients' problem behaviors. Specifically, you wish to learn more about what your patients "look like" when they feel anxious or afraid. You also wish to learn more about the specific situations or objects that elicit anxiety in the child's daily life. To best obtain these pieces of information, you need to broaden the methods of assessment you use.

The first piece of information you are interested in obtaining (i.e., what your patients look like when they feel anxious or afraid) requires that you go beyond the use of methods that assess children's and parents' subjective views. Specifically, it requires that you use a method that allows for the direct assessment of children's behaviors—namely, an observational method of assessment.

In most clinical settings, observing children in their natural environment, such as in their home or school, is not feasible. It is usually not possible for mental health clinicians to take the time out to visit these places and observe. What is more feasible to use in clinical settings, including in your practice (in our example), is an analog observation. In an analog observation you would set up in your clinic a situation that elicits anxiety or fear in the child, thereby providing you with an opportunity to observe how the child behaves. Although setting up an analog observation also takes some work and may not seem practical to you, in our view the extra effort involved is usually worth it, as it can provide you with information that may be lost merely by hearing the descriptions of children and parents. It is sort of like a picture being worth a thousand words.

To be useful, however, it is very important that the analog situation correspond as much as possible to the situations that elicit anxiety or fear in the child's natural environment. To accomplish this, it is necessary to obtain detailed information from the child and parent about the specifics of the child's fear. The analog situation should then require the child to confront what is most scary for him or her. In other words, the situation should represent a test of the child's behavioral limits. For example, in our work with children with Specific Phobia we use a Behavioral Avoidance Test (BAT). The BAT represents a test of the child's behavioral limits as it measures the distance the child can approach the fear-provoking object. Thus, if we are assessing a child with a Specific Phobia of dogs, rather than just hearing from the child or parent what it is that the child does when in the presence of a dog, we would actually bring a dog into our clinic and observe for ourselves.

In using the BAT for children with Specific Phobia, we ask the children to confront the fearful object or situation for a total of five minutes. (See box on page 30 for instructions.) The children are informed that although they may stop the exposure task at any time, they should attempt the task for as long as they can. Because parents may serve as "safety signals" to their children (i.e., children are not afraid as long as they have their parents nearby), parents are not present in the room during our conducting of the BAT. We then assess either the amount of time that they can participate in the task (for a maximum of 5 minutes, at which time we stop), or the amount of distance that they can walk toward the object. We also obtain a subjective rating of fear using the "fear thermometer" (depicted in Figure 2.1).

INSTRUCTIONS FOR BEHAVIORAL AVOIDANCE
TEST (BAT)

Remember I told you that when people are afraid or anxious of certain things they usually try to stay away from what makes them feel afraid or anxious? And do you also remember that I told you that one of the things we are going to help you with in this program is to learn how not to feel so afraid or anxious? You will learn how to face your fears. But before we begin doing that, I need to see for myself just how much you avoid or stay away from [*feared object or event*]. Even though you told me you do stay away or avoid [*feared object or event*], it is important that I see just how hard it really is for you to face [*feared object or event*]. This way I will know just what it looks like when you tell me that you are afraid of [*feared object or event*], and what it is that we need to work on together in this program. Okay?

So I have in the next room [*feared object or event*] and I am going to ask you to get as close as you can (or talk for as long as you can, etc.) [*whatever the particular task may be*] for the next five minutes. I know this is really scary for you, but it is important that you try as hard as you can to do it. If you really feel too scared and feel that you cannot go on anymore, then just let me know and we will stop right away. Is that all right with you? Do you have any questions?

Similar analog observations can be used for assessing children with other types of disorders. For example, children with Social Phobia or Generalized Anxiety Disorder are usually most scared about situations that involve social evaluation. For children with these disorders we devise an analog situation in which they are required to talk about themselves in front of a small group of people (e.g., two to three others) for five minutes. This usually provokes much anxiety in children and provides us with a rich picture of how they behave in situations that provoke anxiety. For example, can they speak at all? do they display eye contact?, etc. A sampling of the types of BATs that we use frequently in our work is presented in Table 2.3.

In sum, behavioral analogs are useful ways to obtain information about what your patients "look like" when they feel anxious or afraid. Devising and using them in your practice may call for some ingenuity on your part. However, particularly for children and parents who have trouble describing the nature of the child's problem behaviors, using analogs can provide useful information and prove very worthwhile.

The second piece of information you may be interested in, as part of your goal to obtain a richer picture of your patients' problem behaviors, is the specific situations or objects that provoke daily anxiety or fear. You obviously cannot

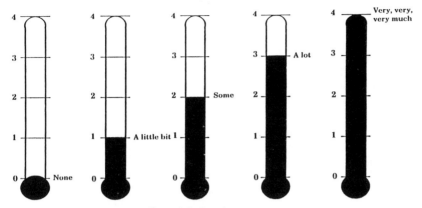

Figure 2.1. Fear thermometer.

find this out by following your patients around every day between sessions! Nor is it useful to merely ask children in session what scared them during the past week, as they are unlikely to remember very much. In our work, we ask children to provide detailed information every time they feel afraid or anxious during the week. They record this information on a daily diary. We ask children to begin recording two weeks prior to the start of the treatment, and they continue daily recording throughout treatment. (This provides us with baseline information that can be compared to information obtained during treatment, thereby allowing us to gauge the child's progress, as discussed in the preceding section.) The children are asked to record each time during the week when they felt afraid or anxious (the place or event), how much fear they felt (on a scale of 0 to 4), their accompanying thoughts, and whether they confronted or avoided the situation

Table 2.3. Examples of BATs

Problem	Task
Avoids small animals (Specific Phobia)	Child tries to get as close as possible to animal and stay close
Fears thunder/lightening (Specific Phobia)	Child watches nature videotape of thunderstorm
Social-evaluative concerns (Generalized Anxiety Disorder or Social Phobia)	Child talks about self in front of small audience
Academic evaluation concerns (Generalized Anxiety Disorder or Social Phobia)	Child takes test
Concerns about separation (Separation Anxiety Disorder)	Mother asked to leave clinic

or object. Copies of daily diaries filled out by children involved in our program are depicted in Figures 2.2 and 2.3.

Of course, not all children fill out diaries as well as these children. Sometimes we work with children who do not fill out the diaries at all, or provide only superficial information such as "Everything was wonderful today!" There is a great deal of variability in the quality of the information provided by children on the daily diaries. Clinically we have found age (older children seem better than younger), verbal ability (more verbal children seem better than less), motivation (high motivation seems better than low), and what one might call "obsessive-compulsive" tendencies (an inverted U-shaped function!) to be related to the quality of diaries. Even when a child does not provide us with diaries or with useful ones, if the child is complying in all other areas of the program, we would continue to work with that child as we recognize that this task may be particularly cumbersome for him or her. As an alternative, we also might think about using a more structured form with the child. Beidel, Neal, and Lederer (1991), for example, have devised a more structured form in which children basically mark on a checklist whether certain events occur and whether they experience certain feelings.

Unfortunately, reliability and validity of the information obtained from children's self-monitoring records, such as those from the daily diary, have not been adequately investigated in research. Despite this, we have found the daily diaries to be clinically useful. The information obtained helps to provide a more complete picture of the types of situations that children find anxiety-provoking, and their subsequent reactions, in terms of their thoughts, feelings, and behaviors. The information also serves to facilitate and to focus our discussions with the children during the treatment sessions.

However, as we have noted, we are not natural-born observers and recorders of our thoughts, feelings, and behaviors, and keeping track of such information can be a real burden and nuisance. Consequently, we have found that it is very important to really "sell" the children on the daily diary records by emphasizing the reasons for their importance. We explain that this is the only way for us to keep track of what has happened to them during the week, which we can then talk about in the treatment session. We also explain that this is the only way for us to keep track of their progress in treatment from week to week, as we are not with them during the week.

We also emphasize specific mechanics about the actual completion of the daily diaries. For example, we carefully explain what each column means and how specific entries should be made. Specifically, under "Situation," we explain that we want the children to write down where they were when they experienced fear or anxiety. The specifics are dictated by the particular problem, but whatever the problem, the children are told to make sure they include all information

NAME:

DATE: 7/17/94

TIME	SITUATION	WHAT DID YOU DO	WHAT WERE YOU THINKING	HOW AFRAID (0 to 4)
9:30 AM	I was in computer class and was copying some disks with this girl. She asked me for the disks that I had already finished, and needed help copying.	I gave her my finished disks and told her what to do.	I hope I tell her the right way to do it.	3
11:30 AM	I was in art and this girl asked me to help to in her project. She didn't understand me the first about 5 times.	I helped her and told her the time.	I hope I don't mess up her project or I'll look like a fail.	4

Figure 2.2. Sample daily diaries: Diary for a child with a Social Phobia (Social Anxiety Disorder).

NAME:

DATE: April 19, 1995

TIME	SITUATION	WHAT DID YOU DO	WHAT WERE YOU THINKING	HOW AFRAID (0 to 4)
8:30 waiting for the school bus	I was outside waiting and my neighbors cat was there.	I ran inside the house to my mom screaming and I missed the bus	The cat would chase me and jump on me.	4
4:30	I was outside and a dog named Cannfleg named outside loose I was nervous	I screamed and jumped and ran in the garage and hid	He would chase me and jump on me and follow me.	4

Figure 2.3. Diary for a child with a Specific Phobia of dogs and cats.

relevant to the problem. This might include who is in the situation with them, what room they are in, what activity they are doing, etc. Under "What did you do?," we explain that we want the children to write down all reactions they may have experienced including their behaviors (e.g., "stayed away") and bodily reactions ("heart beats fast"). Once again, the specifics are dictated by the particular problem. Under "What were you thinking?," we explain that we want the children to write down their complete thoughts, and to take the thoughts to their logical conclusions. For instance, if a child writes down the thought, "I was so upset that I can't handle it," the child would be told to elaborate on this thought (e.g., "I was so upset that I might cry and make a fool of myself and others will laugh at me"). We also explain that accuracy is all that matters, and that there are no right or wrong answers. We also acknowledge that although keeping the diaries may be a nuisance, the information we obtain from the diaries is well worth the effort.

Finally, we tell the children that if they do not have the daily diary form with them when an event has occurred, it is important that they remember the event and their reactions and record this information on the form as soon as possible. It is best that the information be recorded onto the forms as soon as possible after the event to avoid forgetting. To emphasize this point we ask the children if they can tell us everything that they have eaten that day, every song they have heard on the radio, etc. We then point out how they would be better able to tell us these things if they wrote it down right after eating a particular food or hearing a song. Thus, we instruct the children to place the daily diary form in a place where it will be most accessible when needed, such as by their bed if they have fearful thoughts at night, in their school bag if they have fearful thoughts at school, and so on.

SUMMARY

Our goal in this chapter has been to share with you some ideas about choosing assessment methods that will increase the likelihood that you will choose the best method for a particular context. We have also described and illustrated some of the range of settings you are likely to encounter in working with children with anxiety and phobic disorders and some of the range of methods likely to meet your assessment needs. We discussed the types of settings and assessment methods that can be used in such settings in some detail in order to give you a good, solid sense of the range of problems and alternatives for solving problems you are likely to encounter. Some of the common goals in clinical assessment identified in this chapter are screening, diagnosis, identifying symptoms and behaviors, gauging treatment outcome, and obtaining a richer picture of patients' problem behaviors. Although there are additional assessment goals beyond these, the situations illustrated in this chapter are perhaps the most common and relevant to working with children with excessive fear and anxiety problems. We have also discussed what to do if you find yourself in a new or unfamiliar situation, and how being pragmatic helps to organize our thinking about assessment choices.

Although we have discussed our perspective on choosing assessment methods in some detail, the basic guidelines we offer are fairly simple. Our perspective on choosing assessment methods, which is rooted in the "attitude" that helps to define our pragmatic orientation, boils down to these three guidelines: First, we do not let our assumptions get in the way of choosing the best methods. Second, we identify the question to be answered, the problem to be solved, and the issue to be clarified, and then we translate it into a goal. Finally, being pragmatic means choosing our assessment methods depending on the particular goal that we want to accomplish in a particular setting. That is, we choose the methods that will best help us to accomplish our situation-specific goal.

Assessment for Diagnosis

Assessment serves many goals. As we pointed out in Chapter 2, one of the most common goals of assessment is diagnosis. Making diagnoses is an inevitable part of working with children who present with excessive anxiety and fear. Diagnosis is also, however, one of the areas in which you are most likely to experience the type of uncertainty associated with contexts of complexity and diversity. In addition, for many therapists and clinical researchers, making a diagnosis raises issues that are controversial as well as complex. These issues touch on questions that relate to both the validity and the utility of the diagnostic categories themselves, and the procedures used for making the diagnoses.

Our goal in this chapter is to share with you some of the ideas and ways of making diagnoses that we have found useful in our work. We also share with you how being pragmatic helps to increase the likelihood that you will choose the best method for making diagnoses. As in the previous chapter, our focus is on the types of problems that arise in clinical practice with children with anxiety and phobic disorders. We begin the chapter with a brief discussion of one of the most basic issue in diagnosis—namely, the concept of classification, and its utility for therapists and clinical researchers. This will provide a framework for the discussion that follows on the DSM, the most widely used diagnostic system. The discussion specifically focuses on how the DSM is used for making diagnoses for children with anxiety and phobic disorders. The chapter ends with a discussion of the best method for making DSM-IV diagnoses in children.

CLASSIFICATION OF CHILD PROBLEM BEHAVIORS

The classification of child problem behaviors has received its share of criticism, particularly with respect to its utility. Historically, much of the criticism of classification was based on the view that classification lacks clinical usefulness; i.e., in clinical settings classification is done mostly for administrative reasons rather than for therapeutic purposes (Ross, 1980). In addition, many argued that what in fact was being classified was children—not behaviors. Categorizing and labeling children (rather than behaviors) was viewed by many as harmful and stigmatizing (Hobbs, 1975). The categories in classification schemes were also criticized as lacking utility because they represented theoretical abstractions that showed little similarity to the childhood problem behaviors actually being displayed (Hobbs, 1975; Ross, 1980).

Although many of the criticisms about the utility of the classification of child problem behaviors have merit, classification also has a type of utility that makes it useful to therapists and clinical researchers. This type of utility has to do with communication. That is, in therapy and clinical research it is essential to have a common language to be able to communicate effectively about child problems.

Because of the need for a common language, efforts increased through the years to develop classification schemes that would better reflect the clinical reality of childhood emotional and behavioral problems and that would also better meet consensual scientific standards with respect to reliability and validity (e.g., Achenbach and Edelbrock, 1991; American Psychiatric Association, 1994). The Diagnostic and Statistical Manual of Mental Disorders (DSM) of the American Psychiatric Association, in particular, has had an enormous impact on the mental health field, and since its first appearance in 1952 has become widely accepted in the United States as the common language of mental health clinicians and researchers for communicating about adult and childhood disorders.

In this chapter we focus on the DSM-IV and how it is used for making diagnoses of anxiety and phobic disorders in children. Our reasons for doing so are, as you might expect, pragmatic. That is, although we recognize the limitations of classification schemes such as the DSM, and although we think the DSM can (and should) be improved, in the absence of a more useful language for communicating about childhood disorders (at least in the foreseeable future), our pragmatic orientation directs that we adopt what is useful and what works. In this case, this appears to be the DSM.

We thus describe and illustrate some of the types of concrete issues that are involved in using the DSM classification scheme and in choosing the best method for assessing the diagnostic categories it contains. We illustrate these issues with examples that are current and contemporary at the time we wrote this book. We also, however, use these issues to illustrate some of the things that can be done when there are no methods (or at least no viable methods) for accomplishing our assessment goals by describing our work on developing useful methods for diagnostic assessment. We will, in other words, use these issues to illustrate how being pragmatic helps to increase the likelihood that you will choose (or construct) useful methods for identifying children in need of help.

DIAGNOSTIC AND STATISTICAL MANUAL

For those of us who work with children with anxiety and phobic disorders, it was sort of a shock when the entire broad category, Anxiety Disorders of Childhood and Adolescence, was eliminated in DSM-III-R. Within this category, one of the subcategories, Avoidant Disorder, was eliminated, and another, Overanxious Disorder, was subsumed under the "adult" subcategory Generalized Anxiety Disorder. The only subcategory that remained "untouched" was Separation Anxiety Disorder, although it was now placed under the broad category Other Disorders of Childhood and Adolescence. The changes made in the classification of the so-called "adult" disorders were relatively more minor, with the changes being more cosmetic than substantive (e.g., Simple Phobia was renamed Specific Phobia). A summary of how these disorders were classified in DSM-III-R and how they are now classified in DSM-IV is presented in Table 3.1.

Because therapists and clinical researchers who work with children inevitably need to make reliable use of these DSM-IV diagnostic categories, it is critical to have an understanding of how children usually display these disorders. In the subsequent section we thus outline how children usually exhibit anxiety and phobic disorders, and issues involved in their differential diagnosis. To render this discussion most useful to the readers of this book, we focus on those disorders that are most likely to be encountered in working with children. These are the disorders that we have seen the most ourselves in our own clinical and

Table 3.1. Classification of Anxiety Disorders in DSM-III-R and DSM-IV

DSM-III-R	DSM-IV
Anxiety disorders of childhood and adolescence	*Other disorders of infancy, childhood, or adolescence*
Separation Anxiety Disorder	Separation Anxiety Disorder
Avoidant Disorder	
Overanxious Disorder	
Anxiety disorders	*Anxiety disorders*
Panic Disorder with Agoraphobia	Panic Disorder with Agoraphobia
Panic Disorder without Agoraphobia	Panic Disorder without Agoraphobia
	Agoraphobia without History of Panic Disorder
Simple Phobia	Specific Phobia
Social Phobia	Social Phobia (Social Anxiety Disorder)
Obsessive Compulsive Disorder	Obsessive–Compulsive Disorder
Post-traumatic Stress Disorder	Posttraumatic Stress Disorder
Generalized Anxiety Disorder	Generalized Anxiety Disorder (includes Overanxious Disorder of Childhood)
	Anxiety Disorder due to a General Medical Condition
	Substance-Induced Anxiety Disorder
Anxiety disorder not otherwise specified	Anxiety disorder not otherwise specified

research activities and are the ones that most is known about in terms of their manifestation in children.

Separation Anxiety Disorder

Many times therapists and clinical researchers can readily spot children with Separation Anxiety Disorder in their setting, especially severe cases. The children may protest about having to meet alone with the mental health worker. The children may refuse to do so, or they may beg the parent to sit outside the office door. The children may become upset or cry when the parent has to go and talk alone with the mental health worker. A summary of the DSM-IV criteria for Separation Anxiety Disorder is presented in Table 3.2.

Although DSM-IV indicates that children with Separation Anxiety Disorder may also be avoiding school, we hasten to point out that not all children who avoid school are children with Separation Anxiety Disorder (see reviews by Atkinson, Quarrington, Cyr, & Atkinson, 1989; Burke & Silverman, 1987; Kearney, Eisen, & Silverman, 1995): Children who refuse school are a very heterogeneous group. Although a proportion of school refusers refuse school due to difficulties with Separation Anxiety, a proportion also refuse due to other difficulties, such as Social and Specific Phobia or Generalized Anxiety Disorder (described below).

Table 3.2. Summary of DSM-IV Criteria for Separation Anxiety Disorder

A. Extreme and age-inappropriate anxiety in relation to various separation situations.
   1. Extreme and consistent distress in situations in which separation from home or caretaker is eminent.
   2. Excessive and consistent worry that harm will befall parent or loved one.
   3. Extreme and consistent worry of situations that involve separation from caretaker (e.g., getting lost, kidnapped).
   4. Consistent refusal to engage in situations that involve separation.
   5. Steady fear of being alone at home and in other situations.
   6. Frequent refusal to go to sleep without parent or loved one or to sleep over at friends' homes.
   7. Numerous disturbing dreams of separation.
   8. Several reports of having somatic complaints (e.g., stomachaches, headaches) in separation situations.
      At least 3 of 8 above symptoms must be present in the child.
B. The disturbance should be experienced for at least 4 weeks.
C. The onset is experienced before the age of 18.
D. The disturbance should cause clinically significant impairment or distress in social, academic, or other important areas of functioning.
E. The disturbance does not occur during the course of Pervasive Developmental Disorder, Schizophrenia, or other Psychotic Disorder. In adolescents, not better accounted for by Panic Disorder with Agoraphobia.

Children and adolescents may both display Separation Anxiety Disorder, but it is more commonly displayed by children ages 5 to 11 (Francis, Last, & Strauss, 1987). In addition, a diagnosis of Separation Anxiety Disorder is only applicable when anxiety about separation is non-age-appropriate. For example, in infants and toddlers, distress and protest surrounding separation are age-appropriate and are not viewed as a diagnosable problem. In older children, however, if excessive, distress and protest surrounding separation are viewed as diagnosable problems.

Generalized Anxiety Disorder

A summary of the DSM-IV criteria for Generalized Anxiety Disorder is presented in Table 3.3. The core feature of Generalized Anxiety Disorder is excessive worry. For example, children with Generalized Anxiety Disorder may worry about future events, about their competence in areas such as sports or academics, or about seemingly trivial things (e.g., someone misinterpreting something they said). Because all children "worry," a diagnosis of Generalized Anxiety Disorder is only applicable when the worries are clearly excessive and when it is difficult to control the worry. Although this is not always so easy to determine, finding out how the worrying is interfering with the child's functioning in various of areas of his or her life is usually a good way to proceed. For example, is the child worrying so much about his or her personal safety that he or she refuses to be left alone for a minute in any room in the house? Is the child worrying so much about his or her performance at school that he or she cries in

---

Table 3.3. Summary of DSM-IV Criteria for Generalized Anxiety Disorder

A. Extreme anxieties or worries occurring more days than not for at least 6 months.

B Extreme anxieties and worries are uncontrollable.

C. Anxieties and worries are related to at least 3 of the following 6 symptoms for at least the past 6 months (only 1 is needed in children):
   1. restlessness
   2. tires easily
   3. concentration difficulties
   4. irritability
   5. muscle tension
   6. sleep disturbance

D. Anxieties or worries are not due to an Axis I disorder.

E. The anxiety, worry, or physical symptoms should cause clinically significant impairment or distress in social, academic, or other important areas of functioning.

F. The disturbance is not due to the direct physiological effects of a substance or a general medical condition and does not occur only during a Mood, Psychotic, or Pervasive Developmental Disorder.

the classroom the moment the teacher questions his or her performance or indicates that a mistake has been made? Has the parent dragged the child from specialist to specialist because of the child's constant complaints about head-aches, stomach aches, etc., only to be told that "nothing is the matter" or "it's just anxiety"? When we hear stories like these from parents, we right away begin to think that Generalized Anxiety Disorder is likely to be one of the diagnoses assigned.

To accurately diagnose children with Generalized Anxiety Disorder it is also essential to ensure that the anxieties and worries are not focused on specific objects (such as dogs; this would be diagnosed as Specific Phobia), on situations that involve separation (this would be diagnosed as Separation Anxiety Disor-der), on social scrutiny (this would be diagnosed as Social Phobia), and also, that the anxieties and worries do not occur only during the course of Posttraumatic Stress Disorder. Also important is to ensure that the disturbance is not due to the direct physiological effects of a substance or a general medical condition and does not occur only during a Mood, Psychotic, or Pervasive Developmental Disorder.

Specific Phobia

Children with Specific Phobia display excessive fear of a circumscribed object or event that is out of proportion to reality. Unlike adults, however, many children with Specific Phobia do not view their fear as excessive or unreason-able. The types of objects or events that children may fear, and that we have observed the most in our work, include small animals (e.g., dogs, cats), darkness, thunder/lightning, injections, loud noises, and sleeping alone (in the absence of Separation Anxiety Disorder). A summary of the DSM-IV criteria for Specific Phobia is presented in Table 3.4.

What is most disruptive about Specific Phobia is the marked avoidant behavior that usually accompanies it. Avoidance may occur when the child is confronted with the feared object or event, or even in anticipation of confronta-tion. Take as an example the child with a Specific Phobia of dogs. Here avoidance may include avoidance of school due to fear of passing a dog on the way, or of family outings such as picnics, due to fear that a dog will be present in the park, etc. It is obvious how such avoidance can lead to significant interference in the child's functioning.

Like the diagnosis of Separation Anxiety Disorder, a diagnosis of Specific Phobia is only applicable when the fear is non-age-appropriate. For example, in infants and toddlers, fear of loud noises is age-appropriate and is not viewed as a diagnosable problem. In older children, if excessive, it is viewed as a diagnos-able problem. We should note, however, that in many cases we have found that

Table 3.4. Summary of DSM-IV Criteria for Specific Phobia

A. Marked fear of specific objects or situations.

B. The phobic object or event almost always provokes an immediate anxiety response (which in children may also be expressed by crying, tantrums, freezing, or clinging).

C. Individual recognizes the fear as excessive or unreasonable but some children may have difficulty with this.

D. The phobic situation is avoided or endured with great anxiety or anguish.

E. This avoidance, anticipation, or distress significantly interferes with the child's daily routines, functioning, activities, and/or relationships or there is distress about having the phobia.

F. Duration of at least 6 months in children and adolescents.

G. The disturbance must not be due to another DSM disorder.

we needed to be flexible in applying this criterion that the fear must be age-appropriate for it to be diagnosable: Sometimes we have found that a child's fear was totally age-appropriate, but nevertheless, it was so clearly excessive and impairing that there was no way that we wanted to "wait" until the child's fear was no longer age-appropriate before we wished to diagnose and/or treat it! If we did, we would be allowing a child to feel continued distress and suffering, and also miss out on the many activities that render childhood special in the first place.

We further note that at times it may be impossible for the child to engage in avoidant behavior, but the diagnosis of Specific Phobia might still be appropriate. We recall working with 10-year-old Billy, for example, who had a Specific Phobia of taking a shower by himself. Billy could take a shower if one of his parents stayed in the bathroom with him, but he was terrified by the idea of being alone in the bathroom and taking a shower. As much as Billy would have loved to avoid taking showers, this was something that his parents simply would not allow. From the moment Billy prepared to take a shower until the time he was finished, Billy would cry and whimper, and he insisted that his parents stay in the bathroom with him the whole time he showered. Thus, although Billy did not actually avoid showers, his fear of taking showers was out of proportion to the demands of the situation, he endured taking showers only with great distress, and this distress was leading to interference in his and his family's functioning. A diagnosis of Specific Phobia was assigned in this case.

Finally, to accurately diagnose children with Specific Phobia it is essential to assess that the fear is in fact focused on specific objects or situations, i.e., not situations that involve separation, as in Separation Anxiety Disorder, or that are social, as in Social Phobia, discussed next. It is also essential that the fear of the specific object or situation not be a part of a larger reaction to a traumatic event. For example, after Hurricane Andrew struck Miami in 1992, we saw a number of children who came to our clinic because they had severe fears of thunder and lightening storms. At first glance these children may be viewed as suffering from Specific Phobia. A more careful diagnostic assessment revealed that these children were "in the eye of the storm" during the hurricane and were now suffering from Posttraumatic Stress Disorder as a consequence of their experiencing this natural disaster (see below).

Social Phobia (Social Anxiety Disorder)

A summary of the DSM-IV criteria for Social Phobia (Social Anxiety Disorder) is listed in Table 3.5.

The types of situations that children with Social Phobia avoid and that we have observed the most include talking or asking a question in class, eating in the school cafeteria or in restaurants, attending parties or meetings, and participating in team sports. Like children with Specific Phobia, it is the marked avoidant behavior of Social Phobia that is usually what is most disruptive to the families of these children. Also like Specific Phobia (and all that we said about this), a diagnosis of Social Phobia is only applicable when the fear is non-age-appropriate. For example, in toddlers, fear of strangers is age-appropriate and is not viewed as a diagnosable problem. In older children, it is viewed as such if excessive.

Finally, in the differential diagnosis of Social Phobia it is essential to assess that the child's fear is in fact focused on situations that are social in nature. For example, we recall the diagnostic assessment conducted with 12-year-old Jennie, who avoided a wide range of situations. Because the number of situations she avoided was so high, our initial impression was that the most likely diagnosis

---

Table 3.5. Summary of DSM-IV Criteria for Social Phobia

A. The children fear situations in which they may act in ways that bring examination upon themselves by strangers or familiar people, including peers.

B. The feared social situation almost always provokes an anxiety response. In children this may be expressed by crying, tantrums, freezing, or shrinking from social situations with unfamiliar people.

C. Individual recognizes the fears as excessive or unreasonable, but some children may have difficulty with this.

D. The social phobic situation is avoided or endured with great anxiety or anguish.

E. This avoidance, anticipation, or distress significantly interferes with the child's daily routines, functioning, activities, and/or relationships, or there is distress about having the phobia.

F. Duration of at least 6 months in children and adolescents.

G. The disturbance must not be due to the direct physiological effects of a substance, a general medical condition, or another DSM disorder.

H. If a medical or another DSM disorder is present, the social anxiety is independent of it.

was Agoraphobia without History of Panic Disorder (see below). However, we then learned that Jennie, having vomited once in a restaurant (because she had a stomach virus at the time), was certain that she was going to vomit again. The thought of publicly humiliating herself by vomiting in social situations was more than she could bear. Jennie avoided other situations, but all of these had the potential of causing public humiliation, such as going on all-day school field trips where she would need to eat lunch out in public. The appropriate diagnosis in this case was therefore Social Phobia.

Panic Disorder and Agoraphobia

A summary of the DSM-IV criteria for the disorders involving panic/agoraphobia is shown in Table 3.6.

Although the existence of panic attacks and panic disorder is well established in adults, controversy exists regarding their prevalence in children and adolescents. Indeed, it has even been hypothesized that children cannot experience the phenomena of panic because they lack the ability for "catastrophic misinterpretation" of the somatic symptoms associated with panic; that is, children's cognitive reactions are thought to be dominated by notions of external causation, and only in adolescence are the internal attributions characteristic of panic developed (e.g., "Oh, oh, I am going to die") (Nelles & Barlow, 1988). Although an interesting hypothesis, there is no direct evidence that children's thinking about panic symptoms changes in this way. Nevertheless, the occurrence of panic attacks and panic disorder in children is not well established.

In terms of adolescence, among adolescent community samples, 35.9% to 63.3% report panic attacks (King, Gullone, Tonge, & Ollendick, 1993), and 0.6% to 4.7% report past or present symptoms sufficient to meet DSM criteria for Panic Disorder (Whitaker et al., 1990). This has led some to conclude that panic attacks are common in adolescents and that panic disorder also occurs "not infrequently" (Ollendick, Mattis, & King, 1994). On the other hand, methodological problems with the studies that have documented panic disorder in adolescents, such as the failure to use structured interview techniques, have led others to remain cautious about their prevalence in adolescence (at least as described in the DSM), until more rigorous studies are conducted (Kearney & Silverman, 1992).

This is not to say that adolescents (and possibly children) do not have panic symptoms. We certainly have seen enough adolescents (and even some children) in our work to believe that they do. Rather, we are just not sure that the criteria for Panic Disorder in adults are applicable to children and adolescents: Of all the disorders we have talked about in this chapter, we have diagnosed those involv-

Table 3.6. Summary of DSM-IV Criteria for Disorders Involving Agoraphobia and/or Panic Attacks

Panic Attack

palpitations	dizziness or faintness
sweating	disorientation and isolation from oneself
trembling	fear of losing control
feelings of suffocating	fear of dying
choking	paresthesia
chest pain	hot/cold flashes
nausea	

At least 4 of 13 possible symptoms present in the individual, which are suddenly experienced and peak within 10 minutes. Not a codable disorder, occurs within the other diagnoses listed in the table.

Agoraphobia

A. Extreme anxiety associated with situations in which escape might be impossible or a source of humiliation, or help might not be possible if a panic attack occurs.
B. The situation is avoided or endured with great anxiety about having a panic attack, or anguish, or needs a companion.
C. The disturbance must not be due to another DSM disorder.
Not a codable disorder, occurs within the other diagnoses listed in the table.

Panic Disorder without Agoraphobia

A. Both of the following symptoms:
    1. Reoccurring unexpected panic attacks
    2. At least 1 attack followed by 1 month or more of at least 1 of the following:
        a. chronic worry over having additional panic attacks
        b. fear of future implications or consequences of panic attacks.
        c. behavior change due to the occurrence of panic attacks
B. Lack of Agoraphobia
C. Panic attacks are not related to the physical effects of substance use or general medical condition.
D. Panic attacks must not be due to another DSM disorder.

Panic Disorder with Agoraphobia

A. Both of the following symptoms:
    1. Reoccurring unexpected panic attacks
    2. At least 1 attack followed by 1 month or more of at least 1 of the following:
        a. chronic worry over having additional panic attacks
        b. fear of future implications or consequences of panic attacks.
        c. behavior change due to the occurrence of panic attacks
B. Presence of Agoraphobia
C. Panic attacks are not related to the physical effects of substance use or general medical condition.
D. Panic attacks must not be due to another DSM disorder.

Agoraphobia without History of Panic Disorder

A. Agoraphobia due to fear of developing panic-like symptoms.
B. Has never met criteria for Panic Disorder.
C. The disturbance is not related to the physical effects of substance use or general medical condition.
D. If physical illness is present the disturbance must be excessive.

ing panic the least in youth. However, we also have found these disorders to be the trickiest to diagnose, as it is very hard for parents to know if their children are experiencing sensations like panic, and it is also hard for children to describe these sensations. It thus requires very careful probing and inquiry to ensure accurate differential diagnosis.

Thus, differential diagnosis among the panic/agoraphobic disorders themselves first requires assessing whether the youth experiences panic attacks, the frequency of such attacks, and whether or not there is also concomitant avoidance. In addition, with the exception of Panic Disorder without Agoraphobia (which is characterized by the absence of avoidant behavior), one way that we have found helpful in determining whether either Panic Disorder with Agoraphobia, or Agoraphobia without History of Panic Disorder, is an appropriate diagnosis is to determine whether or not school avoidance is present. If school avoidance is present, we suggest that a diagnosis of Specific Phobia (which would be appropriate if school is the only situation being avoided), Separation Anxiety Disorder (which would be appropriate if other situations that involve separation, in addition to school, are being avoided), Social Phobia (Social Anxiety Disorder, which would be appropriate if other situations that involve social scrutiny, in addition to school, are being avoided), or Mood Disorder (which would be appropriate if the youth has lost interest in a variety of situations, in addition to school) be ruled out. If all of these diagnoses are ruled out, then one of the above panic/agoraphobic diagnoses is likely.

Posttraumatic Stress Disorder

Mental health professionals are frequently contacted by parents and teachers because the parents and teachers think the child is "upset and needs help." Moreover, sometimes they think the child is upset because of some specific event or situation. These events and situations, frequently referred to as "traumatic," may include such things as natural or man-made disasters, crime and violence, physical or sexual abuse, and so on. Children who experience these types of traumatic events consequently display certain types of symptoms. These are indicated in Table 3.7.

Unlike adults with Posttraumatic Stress Disorder, children with this disorder rarely experience dissociative flashbacks (Saylor, 1993; Terr, 1991). Rather, children often openly relive the traumatic event through thematic play and direct reenactment, as well as through nightmares and waking intrusive recall (Lyons, 1987). Differentiating between the diagnosis of Posttraumatic Stress Disorder and Specific Phobia was noted earlier.

Table 3.7. Summary of DSM-IV Criteria for Posttraumatic Stress Disorder

A. The traumatic situation was characterized by:
   1. Actual or threatened death, physical injury, or threat of injury to oneself or another.
   2. The experience of the situation caused intense fear and distress; in children behavior may become disorganized or agitated.
B. The traumatic situation is relived in at least one of the following ways:
   1. Recurrent and intrusive thoughts and images of the event
   2. Recurrent dreams (in children the content of the dreams could be undiscernible)
   3. Sense of reliving the experience
   4. Psychological distress when presented with cues that resemble the event
   5. Physiological distress when presented with cues that resemble the event
C. Persistent avoidance of stimuli associated with the event and numbing of general experience identified by 3 or more of the following:
   1. Avoidance of thoughts, conversations, or feelings associated with the event
   2. Avoidance of activities, places, or people that arouse memories of the event
   3. Inability to remember segments of the event
   4. Reduced interest in participating in activities
   5. Feelings of detachment from others
   6. Confined scope of affect
   7. Sense of not having a future
D. Persistent display of symptoms of increased arousal not present prior to the event; identified by any 2 of the following:
   1. Difficulty falling or staying asleep
   2. Sudden outbursts of anger or irritability
   3. Difficulty concentrating
   4. Hypervigilance
   5. Extreme startle response
E. Duration of disorder.
F. The disturbance should cause clinically significant impairment or distress in social, academic, or other important areas of functioning.

CHOOSING AN ASSESSMENT METHOD FOR MAKING A DSM DIAGNOSIS

Now that we have discussed how the DSM classifies fear and anxiety problems, we can turn to the issue of choosing the "best" assessment method for attaining what is most important in a diagnosis, namely, reliability. One thing this means is that two or more independent observers agree in their diagnosis. Reliability of diagnosis in this sense is the sine qua non of a classification scheme; if a diagnosis is not reliable it has no usefulness whatsoever.

Because poor reliability of diagnoses was a major problem in using earlier versions, beginning with DSM-III and with each version thereafter, efforts were made to improve reliability by using more precise criteria for each diagnostic category. However, in addition to using more precise criteria, there is another way to improve the reliability of a diagnosis. This is in the way in which therapists and clinical researchers gather their information from their patients when assessing for diagnoses.

All therapists and clinical researchers, regardless of theoretical orientation, use some type of interview to gather information from the child and parent. However, although all interviews share the feature of being methods of collecting information, they vary widely in terms of their specific purpose and form. In general, clinical interviews are characterized as either unstructured (or nonstandardized) or structured (or standardized) (Richardson, Dohrenwend, & Klein, 1965).

The unstructured clinical interview makes no attempt to obtain information from respondents about the same specific set of issues or problems. Rather, different questions are asked of different respondents, and the questioning proceeds in different ways depending on the respondent's answers (from one question to the next) and on the interviewer's subjective judgments. The unstructured clinical interview is what has traditionally been used the most in clinical settings. However, because unstructured clinical interview procedures generally maximize the role of clinical inference and interpretation in the diagnostic assessment process, the sources of error that may arise are considerable (Edelbrock & Costello, 1984). A major source of error is that which results from disagreement or poor reliability between mental health clinicians.

To reduce disagreement in diagnosis, efforts increased through the years to develop structured (or standardized) interview schedules for use with children. Each of these interview schedules has its own specific series of questions that are asked of all respondents. In this way, "Differences or similarities between the responses must reflect actual differences or similarities between respondents and not differences due to questions they were asked or to the meanings that they attributed to the questions" (Richardson et al., 1965, pp. 34–35).

There are several interview schedules currently available for use in diagnosing DSM anxiety and phobic disorders in children and adolescents. The most commonly used schedules and a summary of their reliabilities are indicated in Table 3.8 (see Silverman 1991, 1994 for reviews). Of the schedules listed, the DISC and DICA are the most highly structured. The ISC and CAS are lowest in structure; the K-SADS, ADIS-C, and CAPA are intermediate in structure.

All of the interview schedules have accompanying parent versions, and most have undergone revision or modification primarily as a way to improve their diagnostic reliability and/or compatibility with DSM-III-R. Work is currently ongoing on most of them to render compatibility with DSM-IV. The interviews are all appropriate for use with children across a wide age range (as young as 6 to 8 and as old as 16 to 18).

Although using any one of the child-structured interview schedules yields more reliable diagnoses than using an unstructured interview, by no means does

Table 3.8. Summary of Reliability Studies Using Structured Interviews for Children

Study	Interview	Subjects	Reliability paradigm	Reliability reported[a]
Chambers et al. (1985)	K-SADS	52 psychiatric outpatients	Test–retest (72-hr. retest interval)	Overall K's of 0.24; K ranged from 0.10 for panic attacks to 0.78 for depersonalization/derealization experiences.
Ambrosini et al. (1989)	Modified K-SADS	25 outpatients attending a child depression clinic	Videotape interrater	Overall K's of 0.85 for OAD, 0.85 for SAD, and 0.64 for simple phobia; K's ranged from 0.53 for simple phobia to 1.00 for OAD.
Last (1986)	Modified K-SADS	81 outpatients attending a child anxiety clinic	Audiotape interrater	K's ranged from 0.71 for simple phobia to 1.00 for PTSD.
Welner et al. (1987)	DICA-R	27 psychiatric inpatients	Test–retest (1- to 7-day retest interval)	Overall K of 0.76 for SAD, phobic disorder, and OAD.
Kovacs (1985)	ISC	35 depressed cohort or nondepressed psychiatric controls	Interrater interviewer-observer	Overall ICCs ranged from 0.64 to 1.00.
Last (1987)	ISC	65 outpatients attending a child anxiety clinic	Test–retest (morning, afternoon)	Overall K of 0.84; K's ranged from 0.64 for AVD to 1.0 for phobic disorder.
Hodges et al. (1989)	CAS	32 psychiatric inpatients	Test–retest (1- to 10-day retest interval)	Overall K of 0.72 for presence of any anxiety disorder; K of 0.56 for SAD and 0.38 for OAD.
Costello et al. (1984)	DISC	242 inpatients and outpatients	Videotape interrater and test–retest (10-day to 3-week retest interval)	K's ranged from 0.96 to 0.99 for videotape intterater; K's ranged from 0.22 for simple phobia to 0.35 for OAD for test–retest.
Schwab-Stone et al. (1993)	DISC-R	41 psychiatric outpatients	Test–retest (1- to 3-week retest interval)	K of 0.72 for SAD; ICC of 0.66 for SAD.

Study	Instrument	Sample	Reliability	Results
Silverman and Nelles (1988)	ADIS-C	51 outpatients attending a child anxiety clinic or the offspring of parents with anxiety disorders	Interrater interviewer–observer	Overall K's of 0.75; K's ranged from 0.64 for OAD to 1.00 for simple phobia.
Silverman and Eisen (1992)	ADIS-C	50 outpatients attending a child anxiety clinic	Test–retest (10-day to 3-week retest interval)	Overall K's of 0.75; K's ranged from 0.64 for OAD to 0.84 for simple phobia.
Silverman and Rabin (1995)	ADIS-C	66 outpatients attending a child anxiety clinic	Test–retest (10-14 days later)	K's ranged from 0.09 to 0.75 for specific symptoms of AVD, OAD, and SAD.
Rapee et al. (1994)	ADIS-C	161 outpatients attending a child anxiety clinic	Interrater (live interview with child and video with parent)	K's ranged from .59 to .82.
Angold and Costello (in press)	CAPA	77 inpatients and outpatients	Test–retest (1- to 11-day retest interval)	Overall K of 0.64 for presence of any anxiety disorder; K of 0.74 for OAD and 0.79 for GAD; overall ICCs ranged from 0.63 to 0.80.

[a] AVD, Avoidant Disorder; OAD, Overanxious Disorder; PTSD, Posttraumatic Stress Disorder; SAD, Separation Anxiety Disorder; GAD, Generalized Anxiety Disorder; ICC, intraclass correlation coefficient; K, kappa coefficient.

this imply that clinician disagreement has been totally eliminated. Moreover, reliability appears to be influenced by many factors. A summary of these factors is presented in Table 3.9. Because reliability is likely to vary depending on these factors, the notion that reliability should be specified in terms of "these subtypes of anxiety disorders for this subject population of this particular age range as determined by this number of interviewers using this type of reliability paradigm based upon this source's interview data" (Silverman, 1991, p. 121) continues to hold.

Because early research indicated that reliably diagnosing anxiety disorders in children was a problem (e.g., Chambers et al., 1985; Costello, Edelbrock, Dulcan, Kalas, & Klaric, 1984), one of the authors did the type of pragmatic (and practical) thing that we advocate doing in the absence of viable alternatives— namely, generate workable alternatives for solving the problem. In this case this involved developing, testing, and refining the Anxiety Disorders Interview Schedule for Children (Child and Parent Versions; ADIS-C and ADIS-P) (Silverman & Eisen, 1992; Silverman & Nelles, 1988; Silverman & Rabian, 1995).

The ADIS-C and ADIS-P represent a downward extension of the Anxiety Disorders Interview Schedule (ADIS) (Di Nardo, O'Brien, Barlow, Waddell, & Blanchard, 1983) and were designed specifically to assist in the diagnosing of anxiety and phobic disorders in children. Organized diagnostically, the ADIS-C/P provides for the differential diagnosis of all the DSM phobic and anxiety disorders and allows the clinician to rule out alternative diagnoses such as Major Depression and Attention Deficit Hyperactivity Disorder, to obtain information concerning etiology and course, and to obtain quantifiable information about anxious symptomatology. Special features of the interview include visual prompts such as the "Fear Thermometer" and the "How Much Things Get

Table 3.9. Study Design Factors That Influence the Level of Diagnostic Agreement[a]

	Expected level of agreement		
Factor	High	Medium	Low
1. Population	Inpatient	Outpatient	Epidemiological
2. Interview interval	1–2 days	1–3 weeks	Longer
3. Sequence of assessment	Neither first	One first	Balanced
4. Instrument type	Same type	Same type	Different
5. Interviewers	Clinicians working together	Lay-trained together	Clinician vs. lay
6. Diagnostic method	Clinicians trained together	Comparable algorithms	Other
7. Source of information	Same type	Overlapping	Different

[a]From Cohen et al. (1987). Reprinted with permission of Williams & Wilkins.

Messed Up Thermometer," to assess degree of interference of the child's symptoms (in terms of school, friends, and family).

Reliability of both the ADIS-C and ADIS-P has been tested extensively. Specifically, interrater reliability (Silverman & Nelles, 1988) has been examined, as well as test–retest reliability of diagnoses and of "symptom summary scores" (e.g., total "yes" responses to the symptoms that comprise each diagnostic subcategory) (Silverman & Eisen, 1992). How test–retest reliability varies by age has also been studied (Silverman & Eisen, 1992), as well as test–retest reliability of each specific symptom that comprises each diagnostic subcategory (Silverman & Rabian, 1995). Reliability of the ADIS-C and ADIS-P has also been studied in other clinical research sites in other countries (e.g., Australia— Rapee, Barrett, Dadds, & Evans, 1994). Work in examining the validity of the diagnoses made via the ADIS-C and ADIS-P has also begun and has so far been promising (e.g., Rabian, Ginsburg, & Silverman, 1994). Taken together, these findings provide growing support for the usefulness of the ADIS-C and ADIS-P for making a diagnosis of anxiety and phobic disorders in children.

A few comments are worth noting here about the clinical application of the ADIS-C/P. First, in our view, an optimal way to use the interview schedules is as templates that guide your questioning—not necessarily as rigid protocols. When we use the schedules in this way, our general experience has been that most families generally appreciate our very careful and thorough probing of the child's problems and that so many of the questions are so "right on."

Second is the issue of parent–child concordance. That is, that there is little or very poor concordance in terms of parent and child agreement on specific symptoms and diagnoses. In Klein's (1991) review of this literature, the conclusion drawn was that "good agreement between parent and child is almost never the rule" (p. 195). This raises the question, What is the best procedure for evaluating and integrating parent and child diagnostic interview information? Indeed, there is no uniform procedure used across the different child interview schedules. Recent theoretical and empirical work suggests, however, that simple integration schemes may be better than complex ones (Piacentini, Cohen, & Cohen, 1992). Thus, with the K-SADS, for example, any diagnosis derived by either the child or parent interview is taken as a final composite diagnosis—i.e., a combination of parent and child reports. In using the ADIS-C and ADIS-P, we have found it useful to use any diagnosis that is yielded by both interviews as a final composite diagnosis. However, disagreements between the parent and child interview reports are resolved by considering both sources' ratings of severity and interference with functioning. (These ratings are obtained as part of the routine administration of the interviews.) Specifically, we have found it clinically useful to view as a final composite diagnosis any problem that is reported by any source—whether it be the child or the parent—if that problem is reported as having at least a moderate level of severity and interference (a rating of 4 or more on a 8-point scale).

Finally, the issue of comorbidity needs some addressing as it is now clearly recognized that comorbidity is common in child psychopathology. This is true when it comes to diagnoses of anxiety and phobic disorders in children as well. Comorbid diagnoses include those of other internalizing disorders (e.g., Brady & Kendall, 1992; Last, Perrin, Hersen, & Kazdin, 1992) and externalizing disorders (see Zoccolillo, 1992). We also have observed this pattern of comorbidity in the children with whom we work (Hammond-Laurence, Ginsburg, & Silverman, 1994). Thus, a key diagnostic issue involves prioritizing the various problems reported. We note that this is a complex task that involves a careful determination of the relations that exist among a set of given child problems (Hawkins, 1986; Voeltz & Evans, 1982), as well as an examination of how these problems impact on the child's larger social context, including family, peers, and school. In our work, we prioritize the child's problems by obtaining child and parent ratings of severity/interference during the assessment process using the ADIS-C/P. These ratings are then used to determine a ranking of the symptoms that should be targeted in treatment. To the extent that the primary target symptoms are something other than anxiety, such as depression or attention deficit, it then becomes necessary to ascertain which of these symptoms, if any, may interfere with the anxiety treatment program. Symptoms that are deemed as interfering may deserve primary attention using modified methods of treatment. Kendall, Kortlander, Chansky, and Brady (1992) provide examples of such modifications in the context of comorbid conditions of anxiety and depression. In general, the development and testing of psychosocial interventions that target child comorbid diagnoses is in its infancy. We suspect this will be a burgeoning area of interest in the years to come.

Treatment

This book is about helping children whose anxiety and distress disrupt their lives and the lives of their families. The effective use of treatment for alleviating distress and enhancing the quality of life of these children and their families is at the heart of all of our efforts as therapists and clinical researchers. The pragmatic orientation we use in our work grew out of our interest in developing effective intervention for helping children, and our growing recognition that effective treatment can draw on many traditions. In the process, we have come to believe that no one particular theory provides the one right way to think about the clinical and research issues, that no one particular technique or method provides the one right way of working with children in distress, and that there is no one right way of doing therapy. We have further come to recognize that the treatment of anxiety and phobic disorders (like other disorders) encompasses a full range of phenomena, and our pragmatic perspective draws on a view of human beings as biopsychosocial organisms. However, although our orientation is biopsychosocial, the treatment approach described in this book focuses on psychosocial aspects, and thus can most accurately be viewed as a psychosocial treatment.

Our pragmatic attitude shows itself in the basic transfer-of-control approach that we adopt in our psychosocial treatment, in the therapeutic stance that we bring into each therapy session, in how we conceptualize, and in how we use specific change-producing procedures and strategies during therapy. In Part III of the book we share with you our ideas about treatment and our ways of doing therapy. Part III is comprised of three chapters. Chapter 4, Building Blocks, provides a brief outline of our basic transfer-of-control approach, our therapeutic stance, and the therapeutic procedures and strategies we use in treating children with anxiety and phobic disorders. Chapter 5, Nuts and Bolts, provides a detailed illustration of how we implement the transfer-of-control approach in a clinic setting. Chapter 6, Obstacles and Solutions, discusses some of the types of problems or obstacles that we have encountered in implementing our basic treatment approach, and some ways that we have found useful in dealing with these problems or obstacles.

4

Building Blocks

Therapists typically treat a wide range of persons for a diversity of problems. One way to reduce the complexity and difficulty of making decisions about treatment is to fall into a pattern of routinely relying on one particular treatment approach. And as in assessment, this strategy may work well with many of the types of problems we treat. However, although routinely relying on a particular approach may often work well, we consider it important to be open to alternatives. Being pragmatic contributes to choosing the most effective ways for treating children because it places no limits on the nature or type of approach that we adopt, other than the pragmatic constraint that it works. Thus, although we (like everyone else) do have preferred treatment approaches, in the end the criterion we advocate and try to put into practice is to be guided by what works with the present problems and populations we are treating.

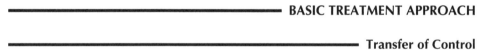

BASIC TREATMENT APPROACH

Transfer of Control

We have adopted the use of a transfer-of-control approach in treating children with anxious and phobic disorders because we have found it useful with all the types of internalizing disorders and in all of the contexts with which we have worked. The transfer-of-control approach explicitly recognizes that internalizing disorders of youth (including anxiety and phobic disorders) are complex, multifaceted, and multidetermined. Four basic, interrelated types of processes—behavioral, cognitive, affective, and relational—are at the core of our transfer-of-control approach. These four processes have long been central to conceptualizations of the etiology of all psychopathology and are the cornerstone of many effective and distinguished treatment approaches. Our efforts in developing our transfer-of-control approach focused on delineating the links between the types of interrelated maladaptive processes or symptoms (behavioral, cognitive, affective, and relational) that provide the basis for a diagnosis of an anxiety or phobic disorder, and the types of interventions (therapeutic procedures and strategies) that can be used to modify those processes or symptoms.

The transfer-of-control approach holds that effective long-term child psychotherapeutic change involves a gradual "transfer of control" where the sequence is generally from therapist to parent to child.[1] Within this approach, the therapist is viewed as an expert consultant who possesses skills and methods necessary to produce child therapeutic change. In treating anxiety and phobic disorders in children, the primary focus of transfer of control is on "controlling" the occurrence and successful implementation of the key change-producing procedure—i.e., exposure. The transfer-of-control approach further assumes that treatment effectiveness is maximized by the use of clear and direct pathways of transfer of control from the therapist to the child.

THERAPEUTIC STANCE

A pragmatic therapist, we pointed out, is defined at the most general level by the "attitude" he or she brings into therapy. The pragmatic therapist, however, is also defined by what he or she does. The therapeutic stance we adopt when working with children with anxiety and phobic disorders has three basic dimensions. It is *problem-focused and present-oriented*, *structured*, and *directive*. The problem-focused and present-oriented dimension is more generally rooted in our pragmatic attitude, although there is nothing in this attitude that rules out adopting an insight and past-oriented stance when it is useful to do so. The structured and directive dimensions are more rooted in the specific nature of the population and problem. Specifically, the transfer-of-control approach itself provides a "natural" structure to how therapy is conducted in that it guides the sequence of the change-producing procedures (from therapist to parent to child), thereby rendering a structured approach more useful. We adopt a therapeutic stance that is directive rather than nondirective because of the nature of the problem with which we work: Anxiety and phobic disorders tend to be linked to external antecedent conditions, and the most effective change-producing procedures tend to involve exposure to the conditions that elicit the anxious/phobic response. Our therapeutic stance is consequently directive because the most effective change-producing procedure involves arranging exposures to anxious/fear-producing stimuli.

---

[1] Transfer-of-control notions of behavior-change efforts have been demonstrated in work with other populations, such as obese children (e.g., Israel, Guile, Baker, & Silverman, 1994; Israel, Stolmaker, Sharp, Silverman, & Simon, 1984).

Exposure is the key "therapeutic ingredient" or change-producing procedure in all of our interventions for *all* of the anxiety and phobic disorders. We use exposure as a specific change-producing procedure because of the growing research evidence that shows it to be the most effective way to reduce anxious and phobic symptomatology (Barlow, 1988). Although there are varying views among theorists and investigators as to why exposure "works," all of these views involve in various ways the modification of behavioral, cognitive, and affective processes (see Barlow, 1988). For example, based on Mowrer's (1960) two-factor theory (i.e., fear/anxious symptomatology is acquired through a classical conditioning process, and avoidance and escape are learned and maintained through an instrumental conditioning process), systematic exposure is viewed as a way to reduce or eliminate symptomatology by extinguishing the emotional arousal associated with the conditioned stimuli. Alternatively, based on Lang's (1977) bioinformational theory (i.e., fearful/anxious images are comprised of stimulus propositions that include sensory details of the feared object or event; response propositions that include the subjective, the behavioral, and the physiological response channels; and meaning propositions that include the interpretations associated with the stimuli and the responses), systematic exposure is viewed as a way to activate the fear image/memory and provide new information that is incompatible with the current fear structure to allow for a new memory to be formed (Foa & Kozak, 1986).

The forms of direct therapeutic exposure we use in our treatments to modify these maladaptive processes involve the child's confronting anxious/phobic objects or events so that reductions in anxious/phobic symptomatology can occur. These exposures involve both *in vivo* ("live") and imaginal forms. Thus, we tell all of the children involved in our treatment programs that they will learn how to handle their fears or anxiety through exposure—"facing your fear/anxiety." Because it is difficult for children to engage in exposures that involve fear- or anxiety-provoking stimuli, in our work (as in the work of others) the exposures are conducted gradually. Most children are reassured when we explain that the program takes a gradual approach to exposure. That is, they will not be expected to face their worst fear/anxiety immediately. We further explain that gradual exposure is used so that they can obtain step-by-step success experiences with the anxious event or object, thereby increasing their confidence and ability to face increasingly anxious events or objects.

At this juncture, it might be worth asking: If we use the same change-producing procedure across all the disorders, what role does differential diagnosis (as discussed in the preceding chapter) play in treatment? Because being pragmatic means using approaches that work, diagnosis can play an important role in designing formats that *maximize* the effectiveness of treatment with children. Hence, despite the common dysfunctional processes across the various diagnostic subcategories (avoidant behavior, maladaptive cognitions, and subjective distress) and the common change-producing procedure (exposure), what does vary across the subcategories is the *content* of the processes. We therefore use the core content of a diagnosis to help guide our design of exposure tasks. In other words, knowing that a child has a Specific Phobia, or a Social Phobia, or Separation Anxiety Disorder simplifies the process of designing appropriate and effective exposure tasks. So, for example, once we know that a child has been diagnosed with Social Phobia, we know that the key change-producing procedure—exposure—should center on situations that involve social evaluation and performance. The specific diagnosis also provides us with guidelines about what might be the most effective pathway(s) for facilitating the transfer of control and also whether other adjunctive treatment strategies might be needed. For example, if we know that a child is diagnosed with Social Phobia we might include the peer group as an additional pathway for facilitating the transfer of control and include the adjunctive strategy of social skills enhancement training (see Chapter 7).

Facilitative Strategies

We also have developed and/or adapted a variety of therapeutic strategies (e.g., contingency management, self-control training) for facilitating the occurrence of exposure. A brief description of contingency management and self-control training is presented below.

Contingency Management

Based on behavioral processes of change, contingency management strategies emphasize the training of the parents in the use of appropriate contingencies to facilitate the child's exposure or approach behavior toward feared objects or situations. A key element of contingency management is contingency contracting.

We have found it useful to employ relatively formal and detailed contracts that are completed each week by the parent and child with the assistance of the therapist. In particular, the contract details the specific exposure or approach behavior task that the child is to engage in each week, when the child should engage in this behavior, the specific reward the parent is to give to the child (contingent on that behavior), and when the reward should be given. We have found that having an explicit contract with this level of detail helps to reduce the conflict and negotiation necessary to implement successful child exposure. These contracts also help instill in parents the notion that they have a primary role in reducing their child's fear/anxiety. (See the next chapter for sample contracts.)

To help parents successfully implement contingency contracting, we give parents detailed instruction and training in child behavior management during the individual parent sessions. We teach principles such as reinforcement, extinction, consistency, "following through," and so on to the parents during these sessions. We also provide training and practice to the parents in implementing these principles both in in-session and out-of-session activities via the contracts.

Self-Control

Based on cognitive processes of change, self-control strategies emphasize the training of the child in the use of appropriate cognitive strategies to facilitate the child's exposure or approach behavior toward feared objects or situations. A key element of self-control training is cognitive restructuring and self-reward.

We have found it useful to use relatively formal and structured methods to help children learn and use self-control strategies. The children receive practice in using these self-control strategies in specific exposure or approach behavior tasks that they are to engage in each week. Specifically, we explain the cognitive conceptualization of fear and avoidant behavior, the importance of exposure to help reduce fear and avoidance, and instilling in the children the notion that they have a primary role in reducing their own fear/anxiety (e.g., recognizing and changing their self-statements, etc.). We also provide training and practice to the children in implementing these principles both in in-session and out-of-session activities.

USING A TRANSFER-OF-CONTROL APPROACH FOR IMPLEMENTING AN EXPOSURE-BASED INTERVENTION

The core concepts and ideas (and the links among these concepts and ideas) we have briefly described in this chapter provide a general framework for our basic transfer-of-control approach. This framework is built on the links that exist between key maladaptive processes of anxiety and phobic disorders (i.e., behavioral, cognitive, affective), related contextual processes (e.g., relational, institutional) that give rise to and/or maintain these processes, and the key change-producing procedures (i.e., exposure) and related therapeutic facilitative strategies (e.g., contingency management and self-control training) that have an impact on these maladaptive processes.

The transfer-of-control approach thus provides guidelines for the general sequence for the administration of the behavioral and cognitive strategies we use. And, as we have noted, in treating children with anxiety and phobic disorders, the primary focus of transfer of control is on "controlling" the occurrence and successful implementation of the key change-producing procedure—child exposure or approach behavior. Hence, when the therapist teaches the parent the concepts and methods of contingency management that he or she is to use to facilitate child approach behavior (e.g., "if the child approaches a dog in a pet shop, then the parent will take the child to McDonald's that evening for dinner"), the therapist is transferring to the parent the knowledge, and the use, of the child management skills that are needed to control this child behavior. Similarly, when the therapist subsequently teaches the parent *and* the child the concepts and methods of child self-control, which the child is to use to facilitate his or her approach behavior, the therapist is transferring to the parent and the parent is transferring to the child the knowledge, and the use, of the skills now needed to control this behavior.

Hence, the transfer of control involves first the training of parents in contingency management and in using these skills to encourage the child's exposure (parent control). This is followed by a gradual fading of parental control while the child is taught to use self-control strategies to encourage his or her own exposure (child control). Consequently, parental (or external) control is gradually reduced while the child learns cognitive self-control strategies in contexts specific to his or her anxiety problems.

As our conceptualization of the transfer-of-control approach has evolved (and continues to evolve) it has helped to crystallize our understanding of effective change processes. That is, we have come to the view that the concept of single and direct lines of transfer of control (i.e., using either the parent or the child as the primary agent of change) as being overly restrictive, and in many instances probably less effective, than a more comprehensive view that includes multiple pathways of transfer of control. Such single and direct lines of transfer do not fully, or adequately, address the full range of clinical issues and problems that frequently arise in clinical practice.

On the other hand, because our approach is contextualistic, we recognize that, in some instances, the therapist may find that it is either sufficient or necessary to work with single and direct lines only. For example, in the case of a young child and competent parent you may find it useful to work directly with the parent—i.e., a line from therapist to parent. Similarly, in the case of an adolescent and a competent parent you may find it useful to work directly with the adolescent—i.e., a line from therapist to adolescent. In addition, in certain settings, such as a school-based setting, you may find it necessary to work with a single and direct line (i.e., a line from therapist to child), because parents are usually unavailable for participation in school-based treatments.

Now that we have described the basic structure and building blocks of our treatment approach, in the two chapters that follow we turn our attention to implementation.

Nuts and Bolts

There is nothing so practical, someone once observed, as a good theory. Theories are sometimes viewed as abstractions from real life. And in a sense, that is what a good theory is. But a good theory organizes some aspect of life in a systematic way and allows us to understand phenomena in ways that we have not previously thought of them and to put this understanding to use. Now that we have outlined our treatment approach, we can begin to turn to the issue of putting it to use.

The core concepts and ideas that are included in our treatment approach provide a general framework for organizing our ideas about how to treat children. Our treatment approach thus provides guidelines that give direction and purpose to our treatment activities. Implementing the treatment approach, however, also involves rendering these concepts concrete and specific and applying them to particular problems, populations, and contexts. In this chapter we outline the "nuts and bolts" of how we have done this. More specifically, we describe the basic structure of our program for implementing our transfer-of-control approach in a clinic-based setting and provide a summary of its three basic phases: education, application, and relapse prevention. The contents of each phase, including the primary goals, are also described. An overview of the three phases of treatment and their contents/goals that we will cover in this chapter is shown in Table 5.1. The final chapter in this part of the book describes in even more concrete detail how to go about implementing each of the three phases of treatment and what to do when certain obstacles come up.

BASIC STRUCTURE

In our standard 10- to 12-week clinic-based child treatment program, we conduct separate child and parent individual sessions followed immediately by a conjoint meeting with the therapist. The first three weeks are the education phase, the next five or six weeks are the application phase, and the final weeks are the relapse prevention phase. However, there is nothing "magical" about 10 to 12 weeks. In fact, our program lasts 10 to 12 weeks for all of our child patients and

Table 5.1. Basic Structure and Contents/Goals of Treatment Program

Education phase
    Collaborative or joint effort
    Learning the necessary skills
    Key change-producing procedure—exposure
    Fear hierarchy
    Out-of-session activities and daily diaries
    Contingency management procedures—reinforcement and
        extinction
    Self-control procedures
        relaxation training
        role of cognitions
        action plans
        self-evaluation and self-reward
Application phase
    Gradual exposure tasks—in-session and out-of-session
    Practice and review
Relapse prevention phase
    Interpretation and handling of slips

their parents so that we can control for length of treatment for clinical research purposes. In practice, there is no reason why therapists cannot modify the length of the program or the length of a particular phase as they see fit. For example, for some families, more practice and experience in applying what has been learned may be necessary. It may be useful to extend the application phase of the program for such families. Similarly, although we see the child for 45 minutes, the parent for 30 minutes, and the two together for 15 minutes, therapists may find it necessary to adapt the program within the 50- or 60-minute therapy session by having shorter treatment sessions over a longer period of time.

EDUCATION PHASE

Overview

The first part of our treatment program is the education phase. In this phase we provide the children and parents with a general overview and description of the program. We emphasize our conceptualization of fear and anxiety and the program's change-producing procedures and facilitative strategies—i.e., exposure—via the fear hierarchy, contingency management, and self-control. We also explain the rationale for the sequence of the change-producing procedures and facilitative strategies (that is—the transfer of control) and the out-of-session activities, and we begin to assign activities.

More specifically, in the parent sessions, the focus is on providing the information and the skills necessary for parents to control or manage their child's anxious behaviors, as well as on how to gradually transfer this control to their child. In the child sessions the focus is on providing the information and the skills necessary for children to make the gradual transition from an external agent of control (parent) to self-control. In the conjoint sessions, the focus is on resolving parent–child difficulties (e.g., problematic parent–child interaction patterns) that are both general in nature and specific to the child's anxiety and phobic problems.

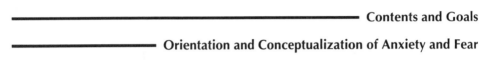

Contents and Goals

Orientation and Conceptualization of Anxiety and Fear

In orienting the children and parents to the program, we emphasize treatment as a collaborative or joint effort among the therapist, the child, and the parent(s). We also orient children and parents to a "nondisease" model of anxiety, i.e., that excessive anxiety is not a sickness or a sign of being "crazy." Instead, we orient them to a learning model of anxiety in which anxiety and anxious behaviors can be "unlearned," just as much as they can be learned. We find that using this model helps nicely to set the stage for the notion that parents and, subsequently, children can learn to control their anxious feelings, thoughts, and behaviors.

We explain, therefore, that children will not be "cured" from having any anxiety, but rather they will learn the necessary skills that will enable them to handle excessive anxiety so that it no longer interferes with their functioning. In this frame, we emphasize that there is nothing magical about the program and that for treatment to "work," it is important for the children and parents to practice the various things they learn in the program just as they would practice any other skill that they are learning, such as playing tennis or a musical instrument.

We next explain to the children and parents about the multifaceted nature of anxiety and fear. We explain the various processes involved in anxiety and fear (behavior, cognitive, and affective) and how these may be seen in terms of child symptoms (e.g., avoidant behaviors, negative or maladaptive thoughts, subjective distress). We tell them that each of these is linked with a different part of the treatment.

In explaining how anxiety and fear are multifaceted, we find it helpful to explain our treatment orientation using a Socratic method of teaching—a method we find useful throughout the program, not just here. More specifically, we pose a series of questions to both the child and parent, such as: "When you feel afraid, how do you know it?" or "What happens to you when you feel scared?" We also prompt, as necessary, to promote understanding. For example, we might ask: "What do you do when you are near something you are afraid of—get closer or run away?" A girl with a severe Social Phobia, for example, might tell us that when she has to give an oral report to the class, she tries to get out of going to school by telling her mother that she has a stomach ache, which in fact she really begins to have! This in turn makes her feel even more nervous and scared. The girl might also tell us that she thinks she is going to make a fool of herself in front of the class and that the other kids may laugh at her. We then, with the girl, draw figures on the blackboard (which we have in all of our offices, but in the absence of a blackboard, a plain piece of paper will do) and illustrate all of these reactions and how they are all interrelated. Because they are all interrelated, we explain, improvements in one are frequently associated with improvements in another.

Key Change-Producing Procedure and the Fear Hierarchy

At this juncture we describe the program's key change-producing procedure—exposure—and its rationale. Very simply, we tell families that when children stay away from or avoid whatever it is that makes them feel anxious or afraid, they get worse. By staying away, we explain, children never get to learn that "there is really nothing to be afraid or anxious of." We explain that fear or anxiety is to be expected in some situations and does not necessarily interfere with performance. What is important is to experience this fear or anxiety and allow it to occur. That is, rather than using initial increases in fear or anxiety as cues to escape or avoid, the children need to recognize the normalcy of arousal and learn that they can experience it and carry on despite it. We further explain that a good way to learn that "there is really nothing to be afraid or anxious of" is to approach what they fear or to do what they avoid. For example, a child who is afraid or who avoids social events such as parties should in fact go to parties. We also give the analogy of "getting back on a bicycle after falling off," which is easily grasped.

When children and parents learn that exposure is the main procedure used and that the child will learn how to handle his or her fears or anxiety by "facing your anxiety," they become even more anxious! They are very relieved, therefore, when we tell them that the program takes a gradual approach to exposure. That is, that they will not be expected to face their worst fear immediately. We tell them that gradual exposure creates step-by-step success experiences, thereby increasing the child's confidence in his or her ability to face increasingly fearful situations or objects.

We next explain how we go about setting up gradual exposures for the child by making up a "fear hierarchy." We describe the fear hierarchy as being like a

NAME: _____   DATE: _7_/_8_/_94_____

```
___/_____/_____/_____/_____/_____/_____/_____/_____/___
   0     1     2     3     4     5     6     7     8
Not scared      A little      Scared of/   Very scared of/   Very, very,
of at all/      scared of/    Sometimes stay Usually stay     very scared
Never stay      Hardly ever   away from    away from         of/Always
away from       stay away                                    stay away
                from                                         from
```

		How Scary (0-8)
Scariest	calling girl on phone	8
	asking girl for her phone number	7
	talking to girl when she's in group	6
	talking to girl when she's alone	5
	socialize/playing w/new people	4
	talking to new people at party	4
	talking/asking waiter/clerk	3
	asking for directions	2
	phone calls	2
Least scary	going to market alone	1
	saying hello (greetings)	1

Figure 5.1. Hierarchy for child with Social Phobia (Social Anxiety Disorder).

ladder that consists of 10 to 15 steps. Each step represents a specific situation or object that the child finds only slightly fearful to extremely fear-provoking. We tell the child that during the course of the program he or she will go up the steps of the hierarchy one by one, and only when the child is absolutely ready to move up a step. Thus, although the expectation is conveyed to the child that he or she is expected to progress up the hierarchy, we also make it clear that it is the child who ultimately determines the rate of progress. Figures 5.1 and 5.2 depict sample fear hierarchies that we have devised with the children with whom we have worked.

Out-of-Session Activities

To introduce the out-of-session activities assigned each week, we explain to both the children and parents that just as the teacher at school gives homework, there is "homework" in this program. However, it is not exactly the same as

NAME: _____   DATE: _____

```
___/____/____/____/____/____/____/____/____/____
   0    1    2    3    4    5    6    7    8
Not scared      A little      Scared of/   Very scared of/   Very, very,
of at all/      scared of/    Sometimes stay Usually stay     very scared
Never stay      Hardly ever   away from     away from         of/Always
away from       stay away                                     stay away
                from                                          from
```

		How Scary (0-8)
Scariest	Holding dog/cat	8
	Being with loose dog/cat	8
	Going into house w/ dog/cat	7
	Petting dog/cat	7
	Going for walk	6
	Petting & being w/ held dog/cat	5
in house if dog	walking to door & ring bell	4
	Being w/ dog/cat leash	4
	Sit on couch alone	3
Least scary	Sit on couch w/mom w/cat	2

Figure 5.2. Hierarchy for child with a Specific Phobia of dogs and cats.

school homework because there are no "right" or "wrong" answers. The emphasis is on trying and doing one's best. One of the weekly homework tasks that will be assigned each week will be an exposure task for the children to perform. That is, it is a step on the hierarchy. Thus, each of the steps listed on the hierarchies showed in Figures 5.1 and 5.2 represents an exposure task that the child would be asked to perform, either as an in-session or out-of-session activity.

Another out-of-session activity that we tell the children they will be expected to complete each week is self-monitoring of their anxious thoughts and behaviors using daily diaries. Specifically, we ask the children to keep track every time during the week that they experience excessive feelings of anxiety—the situation, their degree of anxiety using a 4-point scale, their accompanying thoughts, and whether they approached or avoided the situation. To maximize child compliance in completing the daily diaries we clearly present the rationale for the diaries and emphasize the importance of this task. The details of our explanation for completing the daily diaries were discussed earlier when we talked about assessment (Chapter 2).

Contingency Management Procedures

Contingency management, based on principles of operant conditioning, involves rearranging the environment to ensure that positive consequences follow child exposure/approach to the anxious stimuli and do not follow child avoidant behavior. Consistent with our transfer-of-control approach of change, initially we employ parents as the primary agents of control or change, i.e., as the "rearrangers" of the environment. Toward this end, we detail to the parents during the education phase basic principles of learning, such as reinforcement and extinction. We also illustrate the proper application of these principles. For example, we talk about the importance of following through and being firm and consistent. Thus, in teaching parents the proper use of contingency management procedures, the goal is that parents learn to "control" the occurrence, and successful implementation, of the key change-producing procedure, namely, child exposure or approach behavior. Hence, as we noted before, when the therapist teaches the parent the concepts and methods of contingency contracting (e.g., "if the child approaches a poodle in a pet shop, then the parent will take the child that night to McDonald's for dinner"), then the therapist is transferring to the parent the knowledge, and the use, of the skills needed to control this child behavior.

All of these principles of learning are also explained to the children in the individual child sessions. We particularly emphasize the concept of reinforcement, so that the children can then make up a reward list. The rewards on this list are then used as subsequent reinforcements—given out primarily by the parents—contingent on child exposures during the application phase of the program. We explain to the children the differences among the various types of rewards (i.e., social, tangible, activity), and that our program encourages the use of social and activity rewards.

Self-Control Procedures

Although our initial goal is to attain parental control of child approach behavior or exposure, in keeping with our transfer-of-control approach, our ultimate goal is to attain child self-control of this behavior. Thus, as we also discussed before, when the therapist subsequently teaches the parent and the child the concepts and methods of child self-control that the child is to use to facilitate his or her approach behavior, then the therapist is transferring to the parent and the parent is transferring to the child the knowledge, and the use, of the skills now needed to control this behavior.

Although we highlight in the paragraphs below how we teach self-control procedures to the child, all of these principles are also taught to the parent in the individual parent sessions. We particularly emphasize to the parent that now his or her primary role is to support and encourage the child's attempts in using the self-control procedures that are being taught, and we provide the parent with some ways to do this. For example, we might explain to the parent that if the child continues to seek out the parent when he or she becomes anxious or afraid, the parent should calmly but firmly tell the child: "You know what Dr. Silverman told you to do to help you handle your fear. Go ahead and use that."

Thus, several procedures are used to teach child self-control. First, we teach the youngsters relaxation training. This helps them to realize that they can manage some of the aversive bodily or physiological reactions of anxiety by themselves. Our relaxation training involves progressive muscle relaxation (e.g., King, 1980) and a deep-breathing exercise. Specifically, the progressive muscle relaxation exercise that we use involves teaching the children that "just as they can make their bodies tense, they can make their bodies relax." The deep-breathing exercise involves using a balloon as a metaphor in which the children pretend that their bodies are like balloons that expand when they are filled with air and deflate when the air is let out. The children are instructed to place one hand on the stomach and the other on the chest and to inhale through the nose (blowing up like a balloon), and to exhale through the mouth. Although we have not systematically examined children's learning of the relaxation skills, based on our clinical experience, after about two to four treatment sessions and daily practice at home between sessions, children begin telling us that they find the relaxation exercise "helps."

Our self-control training has a strong emphasis on the children's thoughts and the role of these thoughts in maintaining anxiety, similar to the work of Philip Kendall and his group (e.g., Kendall, Kane, Howard, & Siqueland, 1990). We have adopted Kendall and his colleagues' technique of employing stick figures with "thought bubbles," similar to those seen in comic strips, to help portray different types of self-talk to children. Specifically, we ask children to think of various situations that make them feel anxious and to fill in the thought bubbles with scary or anxious thoughts. We also teach children how to change such thoughts by erasing the maladaptive thoughts in the thought bubbles and replacing them with nonanxious, coping thoughts. As Kendall et al. (1990) suggest, we also model and encourage the child to follow along by asking questions out loud, such as "Is that really likely to happen?," "Has it actually happened before?," "What is the evidence?," etc. The therapist also models and encourages the child to think about what might happen if his or her worst anxiety or fear actually came true—or "what if?" The aim of this procedure is to help the child realize that adaptive alternatives are available even in the worst of situations.

So for example, in working with a child with Separation Anxiety Disorder, we would first help the child to identify situations that elicit anxiety. This might require prompting on our part, such as, "Some kids get scared about being away from their parents just when they know their parents are about to leave the house to go out for the evening. Is this scary for you? What other situations are scary? How about also...?" Once the situations have been listed, we would then get examples of some of the child's thoughts in those situations, such as "I might get killed while my parents are away," and "They might never come back." We then ask aloud various questions—has he or she ever been killed while his or her parents were away?; have his or her parents ever not returned?, and so on. In this case, however, if the child's worst anxiety actually came true—for example, getting killed—it would of course be difficult to realize an adaptive alternative! With humor, we point this out to the child and tell him or her that instead, what we can do is think about the alternative things that the child can do to help reduce the likelihood that he or she would get killed, such as make sure the door is locked, ask the parent to call home one time to check on things, and so on.

Child self-control training also emphasizes teaching and developing "action plans"—things that children can do that will help them manage either the dreaded object or situation as well as their own anxious reactions (Kendall et al., 1990). Examples of action plans include sleeping with a teddy bear for fear of sleeping alone, petting a dog appropriately for fear of dogs, learning social skills for fear of social encounters, improving study skills for fear of tests, eating a hard candy for dry mouth resulting from fear, and using relaxation exercises when aversive bodily reactions occur.

The final component of self-control training is self-evaluation and self-reward. The child's use of these skills during the application phase represents the demarcation of the final shift in the transfer of control from therapist to parent to child. That is, although the children have been receiving rewards from their parents, when the children begin to use self-evaluation and self-reward, parental rewards are faded out as the children reward themselves for successful completion of exposure. In teaching children how to self-evaluate and self-reward their own behavior in the education phase, a list of potential self-rewards, with an emphasis on verbal praise, is developed. Examples include "Great Job," "I really handled that well," "I can handle it if I try," "Good going," "I'm really proud of myself," "I am a brave boy/girl," etc. We also emphasize to the children the importance of self-reward or praise even for partial successes.

APPLICATION PHASE

Overview

The application phase is the second part of our treatment program, and it is perhaps the most critical phase of treatment. It is in the application phase that the parents and children actually begin to apply the information and skills that they learned from the therapist in the education phase. That is, this is when the parent initially, and the child a little bit later, uses what was taught to them in order to control the child's approach behavior toward the feared objects or events. More specifically, this involves first the parents' application of contingency management and contracting, and later the children's application of self-control skills, while parental control (i.e., external contingencies) is faded out.

Contents and Goals

In-Session and Out-of-Session Exposures

In the application phase, the child begins the gradual exposure tasks both in-session and out-of-session. In the in-session exposures, the child is accompanied by the therapist. In the out-of-session exposures, the child is accompanied by the parent.

In the beginning of the application phase, this behavior is under parental control via parental use of contingency management and contracts. These contracts are made up each week at the end of the session, during the joint meeting with the therapist, parent, and child. Contracts are drawn up for both the in-session and the out-of-session exposures. Each contract details the specific exposure task (i.e., step on the hierarchy) to be performed by the child and the specific reward to be provided by the parent contingent on successful completion of the task. Samples of completed contracts that we have helped parents and children to devise during their participation in our program are presented in Figures 5.3, 5.4, and 5.5.

Apparent from the contracts shown, it is very important that they be explicit and that they detail all the precise parameters of the child's assigned exposure task. This includes the *what* of the task, the *when* of the task, and the *how long* of the task. The same type of detailed information is also very clearly delineated on the contract with respect to the child's reward, which is received contingent on the child's performing of the task.

In keeping with the transfer-of-control approach, once the children's approach behavior is under parental control, we start to phase out parental control

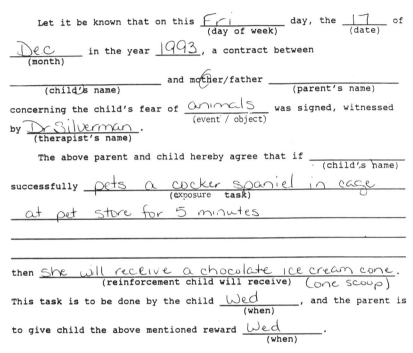

Contract Number __2__

Session Number __4__

<u>Parent-Child Contract</u>

Let it be known that on this __Fri__ day, the __17__ of
(day of week)   (date)
__Dec__ in the year __1993__, a contract between
(month)

_____ and mother/father _____
(child's name)   (parent's name)

concerning the child's fear of __animals__ was signed, witnessed
(event / object)

by __Dr Silverman__.
(therapist's name)

The above parent and child hereby agree that if _____
(child's name)

successfully __pets a cocker spaniel in cage__
(exposure task)

__at pet store for 5 minutes__

_____

_____

then __she will receive a chocolate ice cream cone__.
(reinforcement child will receive) (one scoop)

This task is to be done by the child __Wed__, and the parent is
(when)

to give child the above mentioned reward __Wed__.
(when)

Figure 5.3. Contract for a child with a Specific Phobia of dogs and cats.

(e.g., the contingency contracts) and have the children begin applying the relaxation and cognitive self-control strategies they learned during the education phase. In applying these skills during the exposure tasks, the children use the acronym "STOP" (as in "Stop fear/anxiety"). That is, first they identify when they are feeling *S*cared or anxious ("S") and what their scary or anxious *T*houghts are ("T"). Then they identify or generate *O*ther alternative, coping thoughts and behaviors ("O"), and finally, they engage in self-evaluation and self-reward (*P*raise—"P"). The children use "STOP" during both the in-session and the out-of-session exposures. In the in-session exposures, the therapist is present to

Contract Number __3__

Session Number __4__

Parent-Child Contract

Let it be known that on this __Wed__ day, the __22__ of
                                         (day of week)   (date)

__Feb__ in the year __1995__, a contract between
(month)

_____ and mother/father _____
(child's name)   (parent's name)

concerning the child's fear of __Being alone__ was signed, witnessed
                                  (event / object)
by __Dr Silverman__.
   (therapist's name)

The above parent and child hereby agree that if _____
                                          (child's name)

successfully __waits in living room while parents__
                               (exposure task)

__leave for 20 minutes__.

_____

_____

then __will play tennis with parents__
            (reinforcement child will receive)

This task is to be done by the child __Wed__, and the parent is
                                  (when)

to give child the above mentioned reward __Wed__.
                                       (when)

Figure 5.4. Contract for a child with Separation Anxiety Disorder.

ensure correct application of the acronym; the same is true for the parent during the out-of-session exposures.

We use various prompts to facilitate child recall of the "STOP" procedure. For example, we spend part of a child session having the child draw STOP cards. We tell the children to be sure to carry the card with them whenever they are carrying out an exposure task. We also have STOP stamps that are stamped on all material handed to the child, such as on the daily diary sheets. In addition, throughout our clinic are large STOP signs, purchased at Toys-Я-

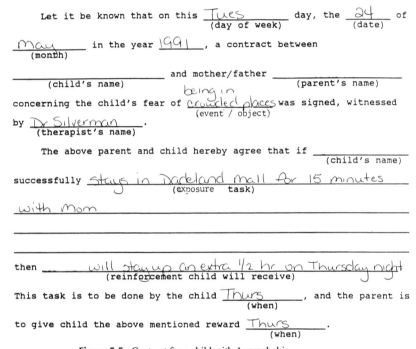

Contract Number 4

Session Number 5

<u>Parent-Child Contract</u>

Let it be known that on this Tues____ day, the 24 of
_____(day of week)_____(date)

May____ in the year 1991__, a contract between
(month)

_____ and mother/father _____
(child's name)   (parent's name)
                              being in
concerning the child's fear of crowded places was signed, witnessed
                              (event / object)
by Dr Silverman____.
   (therapist's name)

The above parent and child hereby agree that if _____
                                                              (child's name)

successfully stays in Darkland mall for 15 minutes
              (exposure task)

with mom _____

_____

_____

then ____ will stay up an extra 1/2 hr on Thursday night
         (reinforcement child will receive)

This task is to be done by the child Thurs____, and the parent is
                                        (when)

to give child the above mentioned reward Thurs____.
                                           (when)

Figure 5.5. Contract for a child with Agoraphobia.

Us. These are kept in the room with the child during his or her in-session exposure task.

Review of Principles and Exposures

In addition to the child exposure tasks, some time is also spent during the application phase sessions in reviewing those principles that were taught to the parents and children, respectively, in the education phase. This is done in the context of discussing the child's performance in carrying out the exposure tasks.

For example, to the extent that a child may have been unable to complete a exposure, it might be important to review a certain principle that was taught during the education phases (e.g., generating alternative, coping thoughts) so that the child will be more likely to have a success experience the next time.

RELAPSE PREVENTION PHASE

Overview

The final phase of our treatment program is relapse prevention. In relapse prevention, specific strategies are explicitly programmed and taught in treatment to help children and parents learn how to handle potential "slips." Training in relapse prevention is included in our program because of the growing recognition that treatment gains are not automatically or readily maintained in child therapy (e.g., Kazdin, 1993). Relapse prevention training is also very much consistent with the "spirit" of transfer of control. That is, in teaching children and parents relapse prevention, the message being communicated to them is that even if and/or when they are no longer seeing the therapist, they will still be able to handle things by themselves—without the therapist's assistance, as they now have knowledge of the skills and methods needed to control child behavior. This includes child slipping.

Practice

To explain relapse prevention, we focus on what children and parents should do if the child "slips." But first, we review and praise the child's progress made thus far and convey the expectation that progress will continue—if the child continues to practice the skills learned during treatment. We stress that the best way to prevent slips from occurring is through continued practice and use of the skills learned in the program. In making this point, we remind the children and parents of all the skills they were taught in the program. As with any skill, such as playing the piano, if they practice regularly they will get better and better at the skill. This will also prevent them from becoming "rusty" and forgetting the skill. In other words, practice will make it less likely that a slip will occur.

Interpretation of Slips

We also explain, however, that slips do sometimes occur and that this is common. A slip does not mean, however, that the child is back where he or she started prior to treatment. The child will still remember all the skills learned. A diet analogy is given to help illustrate the concept of slipping. That is, if a person loses weight on a diet but then on one occasion goes off the diet, this does not mean that the whole diet was a waste and that the whole weight loss effort is now blown. Most children easily understand the diet analogy and understand the parallel with their progress in this program.

We also have found that it is just as critical to review the concept of slipping and its interpretation (i.e., "all is not lost") with the parent. Specifically, we explain to the parent that if he or she expresses disappointment that the child has "failed" because of a slip, it is likely that the child will also feel that he or she has failed. On the other hand, if the parent expresses confidence that the child's slip is merely a temporary setback that can be overcome, it is likely that the child will feel the same.

Case Example

Now that we have described the nuts and bolts of our basic treatment program, by way of illustration we present a case (Louis) we recently treated that is not unlike many other cases with whom we have worked. However, what makes Louis a little different (and interesting) from the "standard" case is that his mother also suffered from anxiety problems and, at times, this made it difficult for her to support her son's exposure efforts. The case of Louis shows how things such as this can influence the basic transfer-of-control approach and how we sometimes need to go beyond the nuts and bolts of the basic approach in order to handle these things. Indeed, this has been a major theme of this book—that things change and that as they do we need to be open to new and better ideas and new and better ways.

The Case of Louis

Description and History

Louis Marks (not his real name), a 12-year-old boy, was referred to our center by a school counselor. The counselor was concerned because Louis was having more and more trouble every day staying in school for the whole day. By around 11:00 in the morning Louis would start looking upset in the classroom, would tell the teacher that he could no longer stay in the room, and would ask to be excused. At first Louis would be sent to the school nurse and his mother would have to pick him up early from school. Because the school nurse says that there is "nothing wrong" with him, Louis is no longer allowed to sit in the nurse's office. Thus, Louis is now sitting in the counselor's office while he waits for his mother to come and pick him up. The counselor is finding Louis' daily presence in his office extremely disruptive as it limits his accessibility to the many other students who need his help. The counselor also is not sure if it is a good idea for Louis' mother to be coming to school every day to pick him up early. When the counselor called us at the center, we told him to give Louis' mother our telephone number and have her call us to schedule an appointment for an initial evaluation. A few hours later, Louis' mother called us and an appointment was scheduled for two days later.

Louis and his mother came in for their appointment, and respective child and parent versions of the Anxiety Disorders Interview Schedule for Children were given to each. Both Louis and his mother reported during the interview that Louis had few friends and hardly ever went to any type of social activities that involved other children his age. Activities that were particularly hard for Louis included parties, playing on any sports teams, and going to public bathrooms, including the bathrooms in school. In school, 10:50 a.m. was when he had Spanish and this was an especially difficult time for him. He really hated having to speak aloud in class and to carry on conversations with his classmates. He reported that rather than thinking about Spanish and concentrating on that, he worried a lot about what the other kids in his class were thinking of him, and this just made him feel even more self-conscious in front of the others.

Ms. Marks, a single parent, also told us during the assessment that she had received psychotherapy and medication for "panic attacks" approximately two years ago. She felt the treatment was generally successful, but she reported having occasional panic episodes and experiences of anxiety—particularly when things were stressful at home or at work. Ms. Marks also told us that she had a lot of social fears herself. For example, she was afraid to meet new people and she also worried a lot about what others thought about her. Other than her immediate family, Ms. Marks had little to do with other people; she told us, "it's basically Louis and me." She admitted that her close relationship with her son had definitely limited her developing other friendships for herself.

Overall, Louis' social anxieties were disrupting the family's functioning and were also severely interfering with his daily functioning in school and social events. Louis was assigned a primary diagnosis of Social Phobia (Social Anxiety Disorder).

Synopsis of Therapy Sessions

During the education phase of treatment an overview of the program's goals and the transfer-of-control model was given. Ms. Marks and her son were also each taught the basic principles underlying both contingency management and, then, self-control strategies. The fear hierarchy was also finalized during this phase. This hierarchy is listed in Table 5.2.

Table 5.2. Louis' Fear Hierarchy

Stay in Spanish class for 35 min and talk about self for 10 min and respond to questions from class; in counselor's office for 2 min, and return to class for remainder

Stay in Spanish class for 35 min and talk about self for 8 min and respond to questions from class; in counselor's office for 3 min, and return to class for remainder

Stay in Spanish class for first 30 min and talk about self for 8 min; in counselor's office for 5 min, and return to class for remainder

Stay in Spanish class for first 30 min and talk about self for 5 min; in counselor's office for 5 min, and return to class for remainder

Stay in Spanish class for first 20 min and talk about self for 5 min; in counselor's office for 15 min, and return to class for remainder

Stay in Spanish class for first 20 min and have a 5-min conversation with a classmate; in counselor's office for 15 min, and return to class for remainder

Stay in Spanish class for first 20 min and have a 2-min conversation with a classmate; in counselor's office for 15 min, and return to class for remainder

Stay in Spanish class for first 15 min and ask a question; in counselor's office for 20 min, and return to class for remainder

Stay in Spanish class for first 15 min; in counselor's office for 20 min, and return to class for remainder

Enter bathroom in school and use urinal and sink

Enter bathroom in school and use sink

Enter bathroom in school

Apparent from the hierarchy, although Louis reported other situations that made him anxious besides those listed (e.g., parties, playing on sports teams), because our program is short-term in nature, it was not possible to include every single anxiety-provoking situation on the hierarchy. We thus explained this to Louis and his mother (as we do with all our cases) and further explained that what we primarily hope to accomplish with the hierarchy is to get them on the "right foot" or put them on the "right path" in terms of helping them learn how to manage Louis' anxiety problems. In light of this, we asked Louis and his mother to identify the situations that should take priority and be targeted for exposure during their participation in the treatment program. Both Louis and his mother agreed that the situations that were eliciting anxiety and avoidance in school—going to the bathroom and, particularly, Spanish class—were clearly the most debilitating and interfering. Hence, as depicted in the hierarchy, we focused some attention on Louis' avoidance of the school bathrooms but concentrated most of our efforts on gradually increasing the amount of time that Louis had to stay in Spanish before he was allowed to go to the counselor's office. The amount of time he could stay in the counselor's office was also gradually reduced; he then had to go back to his classroom for the remainder of the class period. In planning these exposures we consulted with both the Spanish teacher and the school counselor to ensure that Louis' carrying out of the exposures would not be viewed as even more disruptive to either one of them! Fortunately, this was not the case and both were happy to cooperate with us in helping Louis carry out his exposure tasks.

Thus, during the first part of the application phase, Louis and his mother wrote out contingency contracts each week as a way to facilitate the occurrence of the weekly prescribed exposures and to ensure that each will be followed by a specific reward. Initial contracts were carried out successfully, but as Louis progressed up the hierarchy there was increased noncompliance. One unsuccessful contract, for example, required that Louis speak about himself in Spanish for five minutes in front of the class. The reward was to go shopping with his mother for a new tee shirt. On the day Louis was supposed to speak in class, he said that there was no way he was going to go to school. He did not go; instead, he spent the day running errands with his mother, visiting his aunt, and watching television.

In discussing this incident with Louis' mother at the next treatment session, it came out that she believed that having Louis speak in front of his class for five minutes was too big a step for him because he looked "too nervous" in the morning. She further asked the therapist: "And what if what happens to me—my panic attacks—happens to Louis? What if he faints in school or something like that? Then what would happen? I wouldn't want Louis to do this if that were to happen." Due in part to Ms. Marks' own history of anxiety, the transfer-of-control pathway from mother to child was "blocked" in this particular incident.

In subsequent treatment sessions, emphasis was placed on "unblocking" the mother–child pathway of transfer of control. This was accomplished by first pointing out to Ms. Marks how her behaviors were working against the program's main goals of increasing Louis' approach behavior, and she was helped to see distinctions between herself and her son (e.g., "because you panic doesn't mean Louis will"). Ms. Marks was encouraged to discuss her discomfort in seeing her son anxious and her "instinct" to reassure and protect him. The role that her own social anxiety played in this incident was also discussed. Alternative solutions to what we call "protection trap behaviors" (see next chapter) were generated. It was further pointed out that Ms. Marks had "a lot of time to worry" about Louis as it was just the two of them at home and she did not have other activities or hobbies. After discussing this point at length, Ms. Marks signed up for an adult community education class—something she always wanted to do. This helped in diverting some of Ms. Marks' intense attention away from her son and onto another activity, while also helping to extend her social interactions and network and helping her with her own social anxieties. Ms. Marks received additional training in the use and application of appropriate contingencies, followed by more explicit instruction in how to encourage Louis to use his newly acquired self-control skills.

All of these methods were helpful in unblocking the pathway between Ms. Marks and Louis—their subsequent contracts were all successfully carried out, including the one that had previously given Louis trouble—speaking about himself in Spanish for five minutes in front of the class. In addition, Louis informed us that he had just signed up for soccer and had just been invited to a party, which he was planning to attend. He told us that although he was "kind of nervous about it," he was looking forward to these opportunities for exposure. Our telephone contacts with the school counselor also confirmed that Louis was carrying out his prescribed tasks on the contracts, as Louis was staying in Spanish for gradually longer time periods. The counselor was pleased because Louis' time in his office was also now very short and was no longer interfering with the counselor's activities.

6

Obstacles and Solutions

The case of Louis that closed Chapter 5 illustrates something that as practicing therapists you probably have already come to realize. That is, that there is more to know about working with children and their families than the nuts and bolts or the how-to's. (In fact, if you are a practicing therapist, you were probably familiar with most of the basic how-to's.) In this chapter we thus shift focus to the how-to when what you thought was going to work doesn't. We shift focus because this is what most therapists face in daily practice. In working with children and their families, including children with anxiety and phobic disorders, it is not unusual that therapists know what to do, but what they want to do or need to do cannot be done. Treating children and their families is rarely smooth sailing because obstacles frequently arise, as they did with Louis.

As pragmatic therapists, this of course comes as no surprise. As pragmatic therapists we understand that when treating children and families, things change and things come up that may interfere with the how-to. Because of this, we understand the need to be skeptical about the one how-to way. We guard against being smug about the one way and we are open to other ways of doing things when it is useful to do so (e.g., when problems arise). We thus understand the need to think about the ways things change for the worse as well as for the better, and then, if and when these things come up, fall back on our problem-focused attitude and think about how to handle these things.

In this chapter we share with you some of the common obstacles that we have found come up frequently during the education, application, and relapse prevention phase of treatment, and ways that we have found useful for handling them. The case of Louis provided one such example. In this chapter we provide other case examples.

You might recognize some of the obstacles we will talk about as being all too familiar—and not necessarily just in working with children with anxiety and phobic disorders. Similarly, some of our ways of handling them may also sound familiar to you and, again, are not necessarily unique to pragmatic therapists. On the contrary, you will see that we draw freely on many of the concepts and techniques used by therapists who adhere to different psychotherapeutic traditions. Indeed, some of these concepts and techniques are very specific and are clearly tied to certain psychotherapeutic traditions (e.g., token rewards—behavioral); while others are more general and are ubiquitous across various traditions (e.g., reframing/restructuring—family therapy/cognitive therapy). Hence, if we find it useful in a certain instance to use a certain concept or technique with a patient, then that is what we do; if we find it useful in another instance to use another concept or technique, then *that* is what we do. Finally, being pragmatic, we do not think that our suggestions for handling these obstacles are the *only* ways to do so; there are surely other ways as well. However, because for now we have found these ways to be particularly useful, we want to share some of them with you.

EDUCATION PHASE

Obstacles and Suggestions

Motivation

A common phenomenon in any psychotherapeutic intervention is the problem of patient motivation. In child psychotherapy, this might be seen at the very onset of treatment, such as when families fail to keep their first scheduled appointment. This might occur in circumstances in which parents are receiving pressure from external agents (e.g., schools, social service agencies) to "get help for the child" (or else)—rather than because the parents themselves feel a need for help. On the other hand, sometimes initial motivation is very high but waning interest becomes apparent during the course of treatment: More and more appointments are being missed or are starting late due to tardy arrivals. Waning of motivation might also be indicated by greater noncompliance with assigned tasks (e.g., completing the daily diaries, doing an exposure task), or by a greater number of comments that perhaps the child's problem is "not so bad after all." Although there are many factors that may lead to declining motivation, one potent factor is families' realization that the notion of the "doctor curing them" or that there is a "quick fix" is an illusion. When some families realize that change is ultimately up to them (i.e., the transfer-of-control notion of change) and will take hard work and time to achieve, then doubts and questions about the "need for treatment" start to abound.

In handling the problem of motivation, we find it useful to provide children and parents with more education about the nature of childhood fear and anxiety problems. We talk with them about the growing evidence that these problems "do not go away on their own" and how many anxious adults report being anxious "all their lives." We also highlight how the child's problem is impairing his or her daily functioning in terms of school, friends, or family, and how gaining control of this problem will decrease this impairment. For example, in a family in which the child has Agoraphobia, we might emphasize some of the positive benefits likely to result if the child no longer avoids going to crowded places such as theaters, parties, malls, and parks. Or, with a child with Generalized Anxiety Disorder, we might emphasize how the *parents'* lives will improve if they no longer need to reassure the child for every little episode or event that occurs that leads him or her to worry—not to mention the reduced distress that the child will now be experiencing him or herself.

Children also sometimes are reluctant about treatment because they are embarrassed or ashamed about their problems: Talking about it every week in detail is difficult. Although both boys and girls may feel this way, we have found that among some boys, this feeling is even stronger because they have been told (many times by parents) that "only a sissy would be afraid of X" and that a "big boy would not be." In other words, they have been told that being fearful is very "nonmacho." Consequently, many times boys, especially, tell us that they do not feel afraid or anxious, or they underreport the extent to which these feelings cause them problems or distress.

We recall working with one boy, Tim, who was just like this. In particular, Tim, at the age of 12, had *never* slept alone in his own bed in his entire life. After many years, Tim's parents were finally able to get him to start the night out in his own bed. At some point during the night, however, in fact, almost every night, Tim would crawl into his parents' bed. Tim's nighttime fears were causing much distress in the family and were particularly straining his parents' relationship. However, when we first met Tim and talked with him about possible nighttime fears, he plainly informed us that he had no fears.

We thus were faced with trying to learn about a child's nighttime fears from a child who told us that he has no fears. In trying to draw information from him, our questioning thus proceeded in a manner characteristic of many behavior and family therapists and, as we mentioned before, characterizes our own stance when working with this population. Namely, our line of questioning was very structured, and the questions themselves were problem-focused and present-oriented. Below we illustrate our questioning of Tim, which occurred while we were trying to devise the fear hierarchy with him.

Therapist (T): I would like to find out everything about sleeping alone at night that is scary to you—that makes it hard for you to stay in your bed at night by yourself. As I mentioned before, we need this information in order to make up the hierarchy or ladder that I told you about.

Tim: I have nothing to tell you. My parents think I'm scared to go to sleep by myself at night, but I am not scared.

T: I wonder why your parents think you're scared to sleep by yourself at night?

Tim: I don't know. Go ask them.

T: What do you think they will tell me if I ask them?

Tim: How should I know?

T: Well, on the telephone your mom told me that you go into their bed at night.

Tim: Well, maybe I do. But not always—just sometimes.

T: How much is sometimes?

Tim: Like maybe once a week.

T: So one night during the week you go into your parents' bed at night?

Tim: Something like that. Maybe sometimes it's two times a week.

T: What happens to you on those nights—those nights when you end up in your parents' bed?

Tim: I don't know.

T: Well, let's start from the beginning. Tell me, can you go to sleep at night by yourself in your own bed?

Tim: Sure. All the time.

T: So after you're in your own bed for a while, you go into your parents' bed?

Tim: Right.

T: We see lots of other kids who also do that. A lot of times kids tell us that they do that because they start hearing strange noises, or they start thinking about scary things. How about you?

Tim: I am not scared.

T: Could you stay in your own bed if you really tried to?

Tim: I don't know. I never tried. But I'm not scared.

T: What do *you* think it is that makes it hard for you to stay in your bed by yourself at night?

Tim: I don't know. I just get these weird feelings.

T: What kind of weird feelings?

Tim: Like uncomfortable feelings.

T: So at night when you are in your own bed by yourself you get these uncomfortable feelings. What are those feelings like?

Tim: Like I get all sweaty and I feel my heart beating real fast.

T: And what are you thinking?

Tim: I think that someone may come in through my window and grab me and maybe kill me. Or maybe they'd come and kill my parents.

By telling Tim that we see lots of children who do what he does and by telling him how these children describe their experiences, we are, of course, trying to depersonalize and universalize Tim's own experiences. As we mentioned before, this is something that therapists might be likely to do regardless of orientation. Similarly, when it was apparent that we were not going to get far with Tim if we used terms such as "fear," "scared," or "anxious" (either because Tim did not want to admit to having such feelings or he did not recognize his "uncomfortable and weird" feelings as "scared"), we adopted his terms. If we had not done this, the likelihood of our connecting with Tim would have been low, indeed.

Another thing we find useful to do with children who are wavering in their motivation, or who, like Tim, do not admit to feelings of fear or anxiety, is to remind them of our view of fear and anxiety. Specifically, we remind them that fear and anxiety are not signs of being "sick" or "crazy." We also tell them that experiences such as fear and anxiety can actually serve a helpful or adaptive function. We then give them an example, as illustrated next with 10-year-old Sue. Sue's primary presenting problem was a Specific Phobia of small animals—specifically, of dogs and cats. According to the information Sue's mother gave us on the telephone when she first called to schedule an appointment for her daughter, Sue was very embarrassed about her fears. Her mother told us that she was not even sure that she would be able to get her daughter to come in to see us for her appointment. Thus, at the onset of our meeting with Sue, we set out to normalize and universalize her fears. This helps to reduce some of the stigma children (and parents) frequently associate with having excessive fear and anxiety.

T: You know, Sue, everybody gets scared sometimes.

Sue: They do?

T: Yes, we all do. And did you know that fear can actually be a good thing? In fact, if we did not have fear we wouldn't be alive today—we would be dead!

Sue: What do you mean?

T: Well, think about it. What do you think it is that stops us from running out into the street and getting hit by a car? It's fear. Because we are afraid of getting hit by a car, we do not run out into the street. If we were not afraid of getting hit by a car, we probably would run out into the street.

Sue: I never thought of that before.

In addition, our directive stance is apparent at the very start of the program as we explain to the child (and the parent) the transfer-of-control model of change. More specifically, as the next portion of dialogue with Sue shows, we explain how we will initially provide useful information to help her learn how to handle her fear, but ultimately, it is up to her to use this information in a way that will actually lead to change.

T: Also, Sue, don't forget that everybody, every single person in the whole wide world, feels afraid sometimes. The only difference is that some people have learned ways of managing or handling those feelings, while some people, like you, need some help in learning this.

Sue: Like how?

T: Well, that is exactly what we will be doing together in this program. I know some ways to help kids learn how to better handle their feelings when they get afraid or anxious. In the beginning I will tell you and your parents some of these ways—ways that work—that will help you to handle those feelings. But eventually, it is really all going to be up to you. It is going to be up to you to go out and practice the things you learn here. Does that make sense to you?

Sue: Yes, I guess so.

Construction of Fear Hierarchy

The construction of the fear hierarchy is a critical part of the treatment. This is because the steps of the hierarchy will later constitute the child's gradual exposure tasks during the application phase. Before proceeding, we should first acknowledge that the initial hierarchy need not be viewed as a stagnant and final document that cannot ever be changed during treatment. Of course it can. Circumstances and particulars of the child's problem may change, or perhaps the child and parent come to view the problem differently over time. Any of these may make revision necessary.

Despite this, we have found that therapy goes more smoothly when the initial hierarchy has been carefully constructed and when close attention has been paid to the fine details. The fewer the alterations needed later, the less chance there is for later conflict among therapist, parent, and child. Indeed, there are many nuances of child fear problems—all of these need to be carefully considered in the construction of the hierarchy. Below we talk about some of the more common issues that need to be considered. These include:

- eliciting and ranking information obtained from the child and parent
- developing an accurate hierarchy
- handling multiple fears and anxieties and rational ones.

Eliciting and Ranking Information

The initial step in constructing the fear hierarchy is to elicit from the child and parent the situations or objects that make the child feel anxious or afraid and/or that the child avoids. In eliciting this information, we first brainstorm with children and create with them a list of all the different situations or facets of an object that are fear-provoking. Once this list is generated, the next task is to rank-order the items, so that a hierarchy can be formed. Toward this end, we find it helpful to ask the children to first identify the two items on the list that represent the extreme "anchors" for the two ends of the hierarchy. That is, we ask which situation or object on the list is the "most" scary for them to face and which situation or object is the "least" scary for them to face. Children usually do not have trouble in identifying the two extreme anchors. Then, using a scale from 0 (not at all scary/never stay away from) to 8 (very, very scary/always stay away from), we ask the children to rank-order the items (or the steps of the hierarchy) that fall in between.

Part of our efforts in constructing a fear hierarchy with 11-year-old Jan, who presented with the primary problem of "afraid to be with other children," is illustrated below. Described by her mother as always being very shy, Jan now was avoiding going to birthday parties, she refused to join Girl Scouts, and she was spending more and more time playing only by herself or with her 6-year-old sister. Jan's mother was becoming increasingly worried about Jan and was scared that maybe her daughter was becoming a "hermit." Jan was diagnosed as having Social Phobia (Social Anxiety Disorder) using the Anxiety Disorders Interview Schedule for Children (ADIS-C and ADIS-P). Once again, our style of questioning is directive and problem- and present-focused, thereby allowing for a careful and systematic probing of the array of problematic situations.

T: Okay, now Jan, I want you to tell me everything about being with other kids that you are afraid of, or that you stay away from.

Jan: Everything! Everything about it is hard for me.

T: But what is it specifically that is hard for you? Different kids find different things about it hard. If you had to point to the main thing that is hard about being with other kids, what would it be?

Jan: Well, I guess it would be talking to other kids.

T: So talking to other kids is what is really hard for you. Does it matter if it's a lot of kids or just one kid?

Jan: It matters.

T: Which is harder—talking to a lot of kids or just one kid?

Jan: The more kids I have to talk to, the harder it is. I think they are going to gang up on me and laugh at me.

T: What about boys or girls? Does it matter if you have to talk to boys or girls?

T: No, that doesn't really matter. Like my mother wanted me to take arts-and-crafts because I really like art. And at first I got all excited about it. But then my mother took me to the first class, and I looked inside the classroom and I saw all these different boys and girls who I didn't know, and so then I told my mother, "Let's get out of here." So we did. I never went in.

T: That sounds like it was tough for you. Now tell me, how about the age of the kids? Does that matter?

Jan: Well the kids in that arts-and-crafts class that I just told you about—well, most of those kids were my age.

T: So it is harder for you to be with kids your own age?

Jan: Well, everything is hard for me, but yeah, I guess kids my own age are the hardest.

Now that we found out about the types of children that were hard for Jan to talk to, we next were interested in the types of situations and activities that were hard for her. Our next set of queries focused on this.

T: So far you told me that it is hard for you talk to kids, especially kids your own age. It doesn't matter if it's boys or girls, but the more kids, the harder it is. Is that right?

Jan: I guess so. That sounds right.

T: Now, tell me, does it make a difference where you are? For example, is it harder to talk to kids in school or at parties or other places? Tell me all the different places where it is hard for you to talk to other kids.

Jan: More like in places where kids are just hanging out. Like in the cafeteria in school, or when my mother takes me to the town pool and there are all these other kids there. It's just like that arts-and-crafts class. I see all these kids in one place and they are talking to each other. I never know what to do in places like that. I feel funny going to those places. You know how everyone stares at you when you first walk into the room? I can't stand it. That's why I don't to go to any of those places.

Continued probing along these lines made it clear that what was difficult for Jan were relatively unstructured situations and activities rather than structured situations and activities. The more unstructured and the more Jan had to initiate social interactions, the more it made her feel afraid and anxious.

After getting a list of about 10 to 15 situations that elicited anxiety, we next rank-ordered all of them to form the hierarchy.

T: Jan, we now have a really good list of all the different things that make it hard for you to be with other kids. But now we need to go back to the list and put them all in order. That is, we are going to make a list all the way from the easiest to the hardest and everything in between. So let's start first with the easiest. Of all the things you told me, what is the easiest or least scary for you to do?

Jan (looking at list): They are all hard, but it is probably easiest for me to play with a little kid at the playground.

T: And what is the hardest?

Jan (looking at list): It is hardest for me to invite a kid my age over to my house to play.

T: All right, so that is the hardest. Now we need to put everything in between—between playing with a little kid at the playground and inviting a kid your age over to your house to play. Let's start with the easiest and move up to the hardest. After playing with a little kid at the playground, what would be the next easiest thing for you to do? Would it be...?

We would thus complete the hierarchy in this way. After the ranking is finished, we would ask the child to rate every item using a scale from 0 (not at all scary/never stay away from) to 8 (very, very scary/always stay away from). We find that when children rank-order the items in this way, it forces them to really think about their sequencing of items, and thereby allows for the reshuffling of items, as necessary. A copy of the final hierarchy devised by Jan and the therapist is presented in Table 6.1.

We also construct a fear hierarchy with the parent using the same procedure just described above. This provides us with a more complete picture of the child's difficulties. The two hierarchies that are created with the child and parent, respectively, are then discussed during the parent–child joint meeting with the therapist. We find it helpful to write both hierarchies on the blackboard, and then talk about the similarities and differences between the two hierarchies. We discuss whether certain items listed on the child hierarchy but not on the parent

Table 6.1. Jan's Fear Hierarchy

Invite another child my age over to my house while I am at the town pool	8
Call the child up on the telephone and ask the child if she can meet me at the town pool on Sunday	8
Get the telephone number of a child my age and talk to the child for three minutes	8
Get the telephone number of a child my age while I am at the town pool	7
Call the younger child up on the telephone and talk to the child for three minutes	7
Get the telephone number of a child younger than me while I am at the town pool	6
Start a conversation with a child my age at the town pool and try to keep it going for 10 minutes	6
Start a conversation with a child my age at the town pool and try to keep it going for five minutes	5
Start a conversation with a child my age at the town pool and try to keep it going for three minutes	5
Ask a child my age a question at the town pool	5
Ask a child who is older than me a question at the town pool	4
Ask a child who is younger than me a question at the town pool	3
Play with children who are my age at the playground	2
Play with children who are younger than me	1

hierarchy (or vice versa) should be incorporated into the final hierarchy. If the *child* agrees that it should be, we then include it.

Note that we say the child. This is because it is the child who ultimately has to do the exposure. Therefore, the child has to view it as an item that makes him or her feel anxious or afraid, and one that he or she will be willing to confront. Of course, if the child says no, it is important to determine that this is not because the item is in fact a very scary one—one that the child does not ever want to confront! If we suspect that this is the case, we need to remind the child that the exposures will be done gradually, and that this is not something that he or she will be expected to confront right away. We then would suggest putting it on the top of the hierarchy, with the other really hard ones that the child will not confront until weeks from now (after all the other easier ones have been done).

In general, we usually do not have much difficulty in consolidating the information from the child and parent hierarchies. The children and parents typically agree on what the anchors should be (i.e., the easiest and hardest), and although there may be some differences about some of the specifics in the middle, these differences are easily resolved. In fact, it is not absolutely critical whether an item is put as the fourth step or the fifth step. What really matters is that the child feels generally comfortable with the overall structure and sequencing of the hierarchy items. Assuming this is the case, then what becomes most important is that the specific content of the hierarchy items be an accurate representation of the child's fear or anxiety problem. This issue is discussed next.

Developing an Accurate Hierarchy

It is all well and good to elicit and rank children's and parents' information about the situations or facets of an object that make the child feel anxious. Also critical, however, is to ensure that we are developing an accurate hierarchy in the first place. That is, we need to ensure that the items contained on the hierarchy represent the "correct" aspects of the child's anxiety or fear problem, i.e., that the "correct" aspects of the child's anxiety are being increased with each step of the hierarchy. After all, there are an array of elements that can be varied on a hierarchy. Perhaps the two elements that we vary most are (1) duration (i.e., length of exposure time), and (2) proximity (i.e, distance from situation or object). There also may be additional elements of an object or situation that influence children's levels of anxiety. The therapist needs to carefully probe for any of these elements as well.

As we discussed elsewhere (Silverman, Ginsburg, & Kurtines, 1995), one child with the presenting problem of "sleeping alone," for example, may feel most afraid when alone in his or her room—whether the room is lit or dark is not viewed as critical. On the other hand, another child with the presenting problem of "sleeping alone" may feel most afraid when his or her room is dark—whether another person is in or out of the room is not viewed as critical. Two very different hierarchies would be devised for these two children. For the first child, the hierarchy would primarily be made up of items that vary the distance that another person, usually the mother, is from the child at bedtime. Specifically, the beginning of this child's hierarchy might look something like this:

4	Mother stands by the door outside the child's room
3	Mother stands by the door inside the child's room
2	Mother sits in a chair next to the child's bed
1	Mother sits on the child's bed

For the second child, the hierarchy would primarily be made up of items that vary the amount of light in the child's room at bedtime. The beginning of this child's hierarchy might look something like this:

4	Child falls asleep with a small lamp on
3	Child falls asleep with an overhead light on
2	Child falls asleep with a night light on and light in hallway off
1	Child falls asleep with a night light on and light in hallway on

Finally, for children who report that being alone and being in the dark are *both* scary, each of these might be handled sequentially in treatment. The details of this are discussed next.

Handling Multiple Fears and Anxieties and Rational Ones

We handle children with multiple fears and anxieties differently depending on whether we are working with children with multiple specific phobias, children with generalized anxiety features, or children with both specific phobias and generalized anxiety features. In the first instance, we usually target one phobia at a time—the initial target being the fear that interferes most in the child's and/or the family's functioning. We assess this by obtaining children's and parents' ratings of severity and interference using the Anxiety Disorders Interview Schedule for Children, which was discussed in Chapter 3. Accordingly, once we have determined the phobia that is most severe and interfering, a fear hierarchy would be devised for that particular phobia, and treatment would first focus on progressing up that hierarchy via exposures. Treatment for this phobia would then be followed by treatment of the phobia that is next highest in severity and interference. The child would thus devise and progress up another hierarchy for this second phobia. This would continue for the third phobia, and so on. The main advantage of targeting one phobia at a time is that the primary, and most interfering, fear receives primary and immediate attention, and there is no expectation that the child face all of his or her fears at once.

In the second instance, in which we are working with children with generalized anxiety features, there is usually no single specific situation or object to which they can be exposed. This is because children with generalized anxiety features usually report a wide spectrum of different situations that make them feel anxious—though there may be a common theme across these situations, a frequent one being social evaluation concerns. In such cases, the hierarchy that is devised often mirrors the heterogeneity of these children's anxieties.

In constructing a hierarchy for children with generalized anxiety features, there is also another issue that frequently comes up: Many of the fears and anxieties of these children are actually rational and uncontrollable. For instance, after Hurricane Andrew devastated Miami in 1992, a dramatic increase occurred in children's fears about hurricanes. Similarly, media attention to the problem of crime and violence in the community also led to escalations in children's fears about crime and violence. Neither of these fears is completely irrational or controllable, and asking children to confront either hurricanes or crime and violence is neither feasible nor desirable (Silverman et al., 1995).

In handling these types of rational fears or uncontrollable threats, we focus on those situations or activities in which generalization has occurred and wherein the children feel anxious. For example, if children start feeling anxious when there is an approaching thunderstorm, the thunderstorm has become a cue for hurricanes. This situation would be included on the hierarchy and would be targeted for exposure during the application phase. Similarly, if children start feeling anxious when their parent departs from home, parent departure has become a cue for crime and violence. This situation would also be included on the hierarchy, and targeted for exposure.

Moreover, we explain to children that in fact these fears or threats *are* rational and uncontrollable. Because of this, we ask the children if they can think of alternative and more adaptive ways of handling them—besides worrying about them. For example, instead of worrying about hurricanes, what steps might they take so that their families will be maximally prepared during the next hurricane season? Similarly, what kind of crime-prevention steps might be used to decrease the probability of being a victim? Providing education and information is also useful—for example, telling children, "Although hurricanes are uncontrollable, there is always plenty of advance warning, so preparation is possible."

In the third instance, in which we are working with children with both specific phobias and generalized anxiety features, we target the problem (i.e., the phobias or the generalized anxiety features) that is most severe and which interferes most, again, as rated by children and parents using the Anxiety Disorders Interview Schedule for Children. Once we have determined which problem is most severe and interfering, we then would adopt one of the two strategies discussed above.

APPLICATION PHASE

Obstacles and Suggestions

Devising the Contingency Contracts

During the application phase, in which children are expected to begin the exposure tasks listed on the fear hierarchy, the most common, initial obstacle that prevents this from occurring is that vague or nonspecific contingency contracts were written. More specifically, what the child is exactly supposed to do (i.e., the exposure) and/or what the parent is exactly supposed to do (i.e., the reward) if the child does the exposure, is vague or nonspecific.

As we noted earlier, it is *essential* that the terms of the parent–child contract be written in an explicit and specific way. If not, there is great potential for parent–child disagreement and conflict. For example, in terms of specifying the child exposure task, it is too vague to write that a child with a social phobia of going to parties is to "go to a party." Rather, the contract should specify the *amount of time* the child is to stay at the party and exactly *what he or she is to do* there. For example, it might be written that the child is to "stay at Saturday's party for 30 minutes and ask one child one question."

This same degree of explicitness and specificity is also needed in terms of *what* the parent is to do in the way of rewarding. It is too vague to just write that the reward is "to go to the beach." The contract should also specify *when* the parent should take the child to the beach and for *how long* (e.g., "on Saturday morning for two hours with parent"). Without such explicit and specific terms, there will inevitably be parent–child disputes that will interfere with the carrying-out of treatment.

Following through with the Contingency Contracts

In some instances, a precise and explicit contract has been written that clearly spells out the child exposure task as well as the parental reward. But yet, when the child and parent come in for their session, they report that they did not follow through with the contract. There are several reasons why this might occur.

Perhaps the most common reason has do with problems or difficulties with what either the child or parents were "supposed to do."

In terms of problems with what the child was "supposed to do," what we mean is that there was a problem with the exposure task that was assigned for that week. Most often the problem is that the task assigned was "too big a step"—that is, the exposure task is one that makes the child feel so anxious or afraid that the child feels that he or she will not be able to manage it. In other words, then, the steps listed on the hierarchy were not gradual enough. Under such circumstances, the therapist needs to carefully go over the hierarchy with the child and parent and change the hierarchy accordingly; usually this means adding some smaller steps between the steps already listed.

How we did this with a nine-year-old girl (Kim) with Separation Anxiety Disorder who was supposed to "let her mother" leave the house for two hours in the evening while she stayed with her older adolescent sister is illustrated below. In this example, the child made such a fuss that the mother ended up not leaving. This was a typical reaction of Kim's and one that had been going on for the past five years. The problem got considerably worse during the past year, however, perhaps due, in part, to Kim's parents getting divorced and the death of Kim's grandmother, with whom Kim was very close. The dialogue below also illustrates something else that we find often happens—namely, that the child is not always forthcoming in telling us that the exposure did not occur. Perhaps the child feels that he or she has "let us down" or perhaps he or she is ashamed to tell us that he or she found the task too difficult to carry out. Whatever the reason, when we sense that this is what is going on, as most therapists would be likely to do, we need to convey understanding to the child and empathize with the difficulties he or she is experiencing. We also can provide reassurance to the child by reminding him or her about taking small steps, and telling him or her that we need to do that now, that is, do an easier exposure task.

T: How did things go this past week with your mother leaving the house for two hours while you stayed home with your sister?

Kim: Not so good. My mother didn't go.

T: She didn't go? What happened?

Kim: She just didn't go.

T: Sounds like something happened so your mother did not leave the house as was planned. What happened?

Kim: I don't know. She just didn't feel like going.

T: You know, Kim, a lot of times when mothers don't leave the house as planned, it is because their kids really make it hard for them to leave. I wonder if that happened here? Was it harder than you thought it would be to have your mother leave the house for two hours?

Kim: I just don't want my mother leaving me!

T: Having your mother leave the house for two hours was probably too big a step this week. You know, last week we had your mother leave the house for one hour, and you were able to do that just fine. Do you think we should go back to one hour? We can also increase the time if you want, but not all the way up to two hours. It is up to you; whatever you think you can handle.

Kim: I just don't want my mother leaving me!

T: It's hard to have your mother leave you at home. That's why we need to break it down into small steps and set it up so you can handle each step without feeling so afraid. Two hours was too big a step last week. What do you think would be a good-size step for this week—a step that you would be able to do, and most important, that you would be able to try?

Kim: Well, maybe an hour and 15 minutes.

T: Okay, when we meet with your mother let's tell her that. We'll tell her that this week's step of having her leave the house for two hours was a bit too big. So this week we will try having your mother leave the house for an hour and 15 minutes. How does that sound?

Kim: That sounds okay. I think I can do that.

Children may also not have done what they were "supposed to do," not because of a problem with the task itself, but rather because the parent (or parents) is not supporting the child's efforts and may even be sabotaging the child's efforts. When parents behave in these ways we tell them that they are engaging in what we call the "protection trap." This type of behavior was illustrated at the end of Chapter 5 with the case of Louis. In the dialogue below we now show how we explain the protection trap to a parent, this time to Kim's mother. We note that Kim's mother was under much stress herself, particularly during the past year. As mentioned above, she was just coming out from a very messy divorce, only to then have to deal with the death of her mother, who had been suffering for years with cancer. One of the last things that Kim's mother felt she could deal with were Kim's cries and pleas, which occurred even when she stepped out of the house for just five minutes to buy a chewing gum at the corner "Stop-N-Shop!" The dialogue thus also illustrates Kim's mother's growing feelings of frustration and impatience with her daughter's separation problems.

We further note that sometimes helping parents to change protection trap behavior is relatively straightforward. Once we recognize the behavior and point it out to parents, as well as its countertherapeutic effects, parents can frequently change it, with our guidance. Sometimes, however, parental protection trap behavior is not straightforward. Rather, it requires that we take a good hard look at the parents' own history, life circumstances, general behavioral or personality style (are they "avoiders" themselves?), and so on; and only then can we proceed accordingly. This might mean helping parents to gain insight about their patterns of behavior, or as we elaborate on further in the next chapter, providing them with treatment themselves for their avoidance.

In this particular case, it became evident to us that Kim's mother's protection trap behavior was partly related to her own feelings of loss, abandonment, and separation (stemming from her divorce and her mother's death). Thus, we felt it was important to try to clarify some of these feelings with her, and help her see how they were contributing, in part, to her protection trap behavior.

T: How did things go this past week with your leaving the house for an hour and 15 minutes while Kim stayed home with your older daughter?

Mother (Sigh): I'm beginning to give up on this whole thing.

T: Last week was a tough week?

Mother: This is just all too much for me.

T: You've been through a lot this past year. And what's going on with Kim is not making your life any easier.

Mother: I just can't deal with any more hassles at this time. I just want to do what will make my life as easy as possible.

T: So I guess the exposure you and Kim had agreed on last week did not occur? You didn't leave the house. What happened?

Mother: I just didn't get a chance to go. Things got really busy at home—I had the repairman in to fix the refrigerator and then he tells me the great news that I need a whole new refrigerator. Don't ask me how I'm ever going to pay for that! My ex, I'm sure, is not going to chip in a cent for that!

T: Because you got busy with the repairman, you did not have time to leave the house and have Kim do the exposure?

Mother: Well, it wasn't just that. When I mentioned to Kim earlier that I might be leaving in a few hours, she right away began giving me a whole big show.

T: What kind of show?

Mother: You know, what I told you about before, what she always does. She starts screaming and shouting, "You're not leaving this house," and begging and crying with me not to leave. Such a fuss. It was terrible. I couldn't believe it! I can't take it anymore. Not to mention that right in the middle of her show the phone rings and it's my oldest friend who lives all the way out in California, who I know since I'm Kim's age. She called me long-distance. I hadn't spoken to her since right after my mother died. She was calling to see how I was doing. She was worried about me, I guess. So anyway, then I got busy talking with her for a long time on the phone.

T: So Kim's show made it difficult for you to leave her at home, as you and she had agreed to on the contract.

Mother: I just can't handle this screaming and crying of Kim's. My leaving obviously causes her so much pain.

T: You've been through a lot of pain yourself this past year. First you had the divorce and then your mother passed away. And then you have daily hassles like broken refrigerators that you have to deal with. The thought of more pain—whether it's yours or Kim's—is something you would rather avoid.

Mother: That's right, really. I'm just not up to it at this time. Maybe if all of these other things hadn't happened I could handle it, but right now it is just too much for me.

T: I understand. You think if you leave Kim in the house, as we had discussed, that this will cause too much pain. And you don't want to deal with it now. (Pause.) It is hard sometimes to be a parent, isn't it? It's especially hard to be a parent when we have to put our kids into situations that we know are hard for them. It is just as hard for us as it is for our kids.

Mother: I just knew Kim would never forgive me if I left her. I wish you could have seen how she was begging and crying; and she was like shaking all over. I tell you; she was absolutely terrified! You'd want me to leave her like that? How could I do such a thing to her?

T: It is not unusual for parents to have a hard time putting their children in situations that we know are hard for them—that we know may make our kids feel uncomfortable and get upset, and maybe even cause some pain. As parents our instincts are to protect our children from these uncomfortable feelings. So how we might do this—how we try to protect our children—is by keeping them away from situations that we know make them feel anxious or uncomfortable. In this program, we see parents doing this a lot. They give up when their children show any hesitation about doing their exposure. And in Kim's case, it wasn't even a mild hesitation. It was a full-blown anxiety attack. It sounds like you're trying to protect Kim from uncomfortable feelings, or what you think will cause her pain (as well as yourself). I wonder if this might largely explain why the exposure didn't take place.

Mother: Well, it's true I didn't push it too much, and then I just got busy talking with my friend.

T: You wanted to "protect" Kim from feeling uncomfortable or getting too upset.

Mother: I just know how terrible I would feel if someone was going to leave me.

Following this probing of Kim's mother's feelings and how these feelings contributed to her protection trap behaviors, the session ended as follows.

T: So now you understand that that was the next step on the hierarchy, and Kim was feeling like she was ready for this step. It might have been hard, but Kim was at least ready to try it.

Mother: I guess I shouldn't have given in so easily.

T: That's right. You see, giving in, and not encouraging the exposure because you are concerned that Kim might get too upset is sort of like a "trap." It is a trap because in the short term you and Kim come to feel better. You feel better because you are protecting Kim from feeling uncomfortable or scared, and Kim feels better because she will not have to feel uncomfortable or scared. But you see, keeping Kim away from doing this is completely against what we try to do in this program. That is, what we try to do in the program is to get children to expose themselves to what they are afraid of, not to stay away. So in the long term, keeping Kim away is not going to solve anything, and may even make the problem worse.

As we indicated above, once we point out to parents, as we did to Kim's mother, that the protection trap is countertherapeutic, and how in some instances it may serve to satisfy some of the parents' own needs, most are able to modify this unwanted parental behavior. Unfortunately, however, there are those parents who, no matter how much we emphasize the problems in engaging in the protection trap, continue to engage in this behavior. These are the parents in whom the pathway of transfer of control (from therapist to parent to child) is so severely "blocked" that greater efforts are needed to unblock the pathway. In the next chapter we elaborate on how we might do this.

Another reason why there might have been a failure in following through with the contingency contracts is because of problems or difficulties with what the parent was "supposed to do," in terms of giving the child the reward, even though the child did the exposure task. A common reason why parents do not give the reward to the child is because the reward listed on the contract is viewed by the parents as being inappropriate (i.e., too extravagant), but the parent did not mention this during the writing up of the contract in session. In our work, when we suspect that parents are feeling this way, or when rewards being agreed on are too extravagant (e.g., a trip to Disney World, a compact disk player), we intervene, emphasize social (e.g., special time with a relative or friend) and activity (e.g., playing a game, going bowling) rewards, and highlight the need for collaboration between child and parent in order to achieve the program's goals.

However, we have worked with children and parents who, despite our attempts to intervene and our protests, agree in the session on extravagant and expensive rewards. This may occur because for some child–parent dyads, agreeing on a weekly reward escalates into a weekly power struggle, and in turn, to the parent "giving in" to the child's demand for an inappropriate reward. Once again, the pathway of transfer of control is blocked in these families. Positive change is unlikely to occur unless the pathway is unblocked and parents and children define and clarify their respective roles in the family. This too is elaborated on in the next chapter.

Another reason cited frequently by parents for not giving their child the reward is because they were "too busy" during the week, especially if the reward is an activity, such as going to a movie. Alternatively, parents claim that they "forgot." We handle both instances by using a common behavioral technique— namely, we suggest that the parents provide the child with a token, such as a penny or an I.O.U. card, immediately following the child's successful performance of the exposure task. The child is to cash in the token at a later time. In this way, the reward can be earned by the child when the family is not so busy and the parent now does not forget. We have found that using tokens in this way helps parents to follow through better with their part of the agreement.

When tokens do not work and parents are still not following through, we find it necessary to review with them their own motivation for continuing with the program, and what child change (or lack thereof) might mean for them. Once again, this might also raise the issue about a blocked pathway of control and whether, perhaps, we should rely less on using the parent as a line of transfer. Rather, perhaps we should count more on a direct line of transfer to the child (i.e., therapist to child), or on opening up other lines of control (e.g., peer group). (See next chapter.)

Yet another reason why parents do not follow through with their "part of the deal" as indicated on the contract is because they are confused about how to handle the child's only partial completion of the exposure task. That is, the child took a step in the "right" direction, but did not completely do the task specified on the contract. For example, the contract specified that the child was to go to a playground and play with other children for 30 minutes, but the child stayed for only 20 minutes and played by him- or herself. In such situations, we tell parents that because our program rests on the notion of "taking small steps," reinforcement should be provided for all successful approximations—perfect performance is not expected. However, we suggest that the parent provide an alternative reward rather than the one specified on the original contract.

Further, when the child shows only partial completion of an exposure task, as in the above example, it usually means that the step was "too large." We thus need to go back and review the hierarchy with the child, in the way illustrated previously with Kim, and ensure that the child's hierarchy is comprised of enough small steps. In this way, the child will not have to create his or her own smaller step at the time of the exposure task—which is basically what the child is doing when showing partial rather than full completion of an exposure task.

Implementation of STOP

In handling the obstacles that arise in the use of STOP, we adopt many of the suggestions of cognitive-behavior therapists such as Philip Kendall and colleagues (1990). For example, for children who have trouble identifying when they are feeling scared or anxious ("S"), we review the three ways that anxiety is manifested as outlined in the education phase. Some children also have trouble identifying or recognizing their scary or anxious thoughts or behaviors ("T"). To help children with "T," we first ask the children to practice identifying their thoughts in neutral situations, so that they obtain experience with this technique without any anxiety. Like Kendall et al. (1990), we draw a stick figure with an empty thought bubble of a youngster at a birthday party and ask the children to fill in the thought bubble (e.g., "Wow, look at all the presents," "I'm so happy"). We use a similar procedure to help children identify thoughts in anxiety-provoking situations in general, but not specific to their own anxiety problem.

This procedure is then used to help children identify their own thoughts in the fear- or anxiety-provoking situations specific to them. A series of questions is also usually helpful, such as, "What would be the worst thing that could happen?" or "Imagine yourself facing that situation/object; what are you thinking about?" The therapist may also assist by suggesting possible anxious thoughts to the children, particularly the kinds of thoughts other children with similar anxieties typically report. For example, for a child with Separation Anxiety Disorder, we might say something like: "You know, a lot of kids who are afraid about being left by themselves think they might get kidnapped or killed. Are these like some of your thoughts?" Giving examples of the thoughts of other children in this way thereby "gives permission" for children to report certain thoughts and indicates that they are not alone in having such thoughts.

To help children with "O," we also take a structured and direct stance by helping them to identify or generate alternative, coping thoughts. Although we may guide children in focusing on positive aspects of themselves (e.g., "I'm brave and strong and I can handle it") or the situation (e.g., "The beach is a fun place to play"), we especially focus on the "non-negative" aspects of themselves or the situation (Kanfer, Karoly, & Newman, 1975; Kendall & Chansky, 1991). In other words, rather than merely emphasizing the use of positive cognitive strategies, we emphasize *not* using negative cognitive strategies, i.e.—"the power of non-negative thinking."

We use cognitive procedures recommended by Beck and Emery (1985), Kendall et al. (1990), and others to help children with this, such as a series of questions that center on reality checking. For example, for children with a phobia of going swimming in the ocean we might have them ask aloud questions such as, "Have I ever been stung from a jellyfish and if so, how often?" We also demonstrate "decatastrophizing" under such circumstances, such as, "Will I die or be paralyzed forever?," as well as problem solving, such as, "What if I do get stung from a jellyfish, what can I do in that situation?"

The final step of STOP is for children to engage in self-evaluation and self-reward (praise). We have found that many children with excessive anxiety or fear have trouble doing this last step. Its importance therefore needs to be emphasized. We do this via a series of analogies. For example, using a soccer game, we might explain that upon making a goal, a child may react in one of two ways: (1) "Wow, I did great; next time I'm going to do even better," or (2) "Oh darn, I only made one goal; I'm a bad soccer player, I should just give it up." The therapist then discusses with the child the different implications these two reactions are likely to have on subsequent feelings and behavior. That is, the first reaction is likely to lead to the child feeling successful and optimistic and thus, continued playing; the second reaction is likely to lead to the child feeling unsuccessful and pessimistic; and thus, discontinued playing. Most children readily understand how the use of self-evaluation and praise in the soccer analogy relates to the use of self-evaluation and praise in encountering fearful objects or situations—that is, if they use self-evaluation and reward they are likely to feel successful, and thus, continue practicing exposure and using STOP.

As with the use of parental reward, we find it important to also emphasize to children that they should praise themselves even for partial successes and that perfect performance is not always expected or possible. For example, if they planned on staying at a playground for 30 minutes and stayed for 15 minutes, they should still praise themselves for going to the playground and for staying as long as possible (e.g., "Well at least I stayed for 15 minutes. Next time I will stay longer. What's important is that I tried my best").

Mastering the use of STOP is difficult for some children, particularly those who are uncomfortable about disclosing their thoughts. The following dialogue illustrates some of the difficulties 11-year-old Joe experienced in learning the STOP procedure (Silverman et al., 1995). The dialogue also illustrates something that is universal to any type of child work: Sometimes, our child patients display noncompliance and start "testing the limits." In such instances, we would do as we would with any other type of child case; we would remain firm and not allow the child to manipulate or control the session.

> Therapist (T): Let's practice *STOP* as though you were in the school cafeteria.
>
> Joe: I walk into the cafeteria and say "stop" to myself.
>
> T: I mean, let's practice each letter of *STOP* and go over what it stands for and how you can use it to help you not feel so scared in the cafeteria.
>
> Joe: I just say "stop," "stop," "stop."
>
> T: Yes, you say "stop" to remind you what to do...but what does each letter stand for? What does *S* stand for?
>
> Joe: Scared.

T: Right. And how do you know you are feeling scared before you walk into the cafeteria?

Joe: Oh, when I have to go into the cafeteria I feel sick to my stomach, like I'm going to throw up—that's how I know I'm scared.

T: Great, so that is your *S*. Let's write this on the board. Okay, now what does *T* stand for?

Joe: Thinking, but I know all this. I don't need to say it out loud. I'll just practice it on my own.

T: I'm glad you want to practice on your own. The more you practice, the better you'll get. Let's practice together now, and you can practice alone at home.

Joe: I already know how to do it. I don't need any more practice and I don't want to say it out loud. I'll just do it in my head.

T: I guess you think that I might think something bad about you if I hear your thoughts.

Joe: Yeah, you're going to think it's stupid.

T: Being scared isn't stupid; everyone feels scared about something. But your scary feelings are messing things up for you, stopping you from being with other kids and making friends. To stop feeling so scared we need to practice together.

Joe: But I don't see why I just can't do it all in my head. Why do I have to say it out loud?

T: If I was teaching you how to play the piano we couldn't just spend the lesson having you *think* about playing notes to a piece. I would need to hear how you play out loud. This way I can tell for sure whether you are playing all the right notes. Same here—practicing out loud is like making sure you are hitting the right notes. Okay? So let's hear the "*T*" note. What is your "*T*"?

Joe: I'm thinking that the other kids are staring at me and everyone will tease me and laugh at me and I want to leave. That's my "*T*" note.

T: Great. You did the "*S*" and "*T*" part of *STOP* really well. Now what about the "*O*"? What are the "*O*" or other thoughts or things you can do?

Joe: Everyone is eating their lunch so they are probably not staring at me and if I hear them laugh it doesn't mean they are laughing at me; no one has teased me before. But even if they do I can handle it. I can face it. I'm brave. The cafeteria may have something good to eat, too! That's my "*O*."

T: You're hitting all the right notes! What about other things that you can do? Do you have an action plan that you can do when you are in the cafeteria?

Joe: I can ask Billy to eat lunch with me or I can bring a book and read if I don't have anyone to eat lunch with.

T: Very good. Now what about the "*P*"? How can you praise yourself?

Joe: My "*P*" is great job! I did it! I'm really doing good!

RELAPSE PREVENTION PHASE

Obstacles and Suggestions

Termination

Many of the obstacles that arise during the final phase of treatment are those associated with termination issues, in general, of psychotherapy (e.g., Teyber, 1988). Because our program is time-limited, wherein participants are told from the onset that they should expect treatment to last approximately 10 to 12 weeks, termination issues in our work are not as complex.

Nonetheless, termination is still generally a hard issue for many children and parents. To help ease the transition, we remind the families as early as three weeks prior to the last session that termination is coming up, and we keep reminding them of this in the interim weeks. This allows ample time to discuss children's and parents' feelings or concerns about ending treatment.

We show empathy and understanding that ending therapy is hard and that we also will miss them. However, we are confident that the child and parent are now ready to "go it alone." In particular, we emphasize to them that the final transfer of control has now occurred; that is, they have learned and are now using what we had taught them about how to control child anxiety and avoidant behavior. It is up to them to keep on practicing all they learned.

Occasionally, we see an increase in certain problems in some families at the final phase of treatment, even in families where great strides were made. Perhaps the two most common problems we see are increased slipping and increased appearance of other child problem behaviors.

Increased Slipping

Prior to termination, some children show an increase in their slips. For example, situations that children had apparently mastered earlier in the program are now reported as being difficult to handle. Children might report feelings of frustration and distress because of these slips, and they are not so sure they ever really handled these situations very well in the first place.

As caring human beings perhaps our first gut reaction is to tell these children not to worry and they can keep seeing us for the rest of their lives—we will always be there for them! But as therapists, we need to remind ourselves of what we had set out to do and what we now need to do as we approach termination—namely, we had set out to transfer our knowledge of the methods and skills needed to control child avoidance/approach behavior to situations and objects that make the child feel anxious, and we have helped the child in learning how to use this control (via self-control).

Now that we have transferred this control from ourselves to the parent to the child, we need to relinquish at the end of treatment any final control we may have, or that the child or parent may think we have! Specifically, we need to reiterate to the child that he or she now has the skills to control his or her anxiety and avoidance behavior. We need to reiterate this point to the parent as well. That is, we need to remind the parent that she now has the knowledge and skills needed to control this behavior in the child, and more importantly, in transferring this control to the child, if she needs to do so again (i.e., in case she needs to control this behavior via contingency contracting, and then fade this out while the child uses the self-control skills).

Overall, then, we stress the need for the child to continue to engage in exposure using self-control strategies, and for the parent to continue to encourage the child's use of these strategies. Moreover, we stress to parents the transfer-of-control model that guided the rationale and sequence for the teaching of these strategies. Finally, we find it worthwhile to point out that the amount of exposures should increase if the child's avoidant behaviors increase.

Appearance of Other Problem Behaviors

In addition to children showing an increase in slipping, they may also show an increase in their display of other problems. Or they (or their parents) may begin talking in session about a variety of other problems, some of which may be anxiety-related but some of which may be completely unrelated to anxiety and be a completely new set of problems. When this happens we need to once again discuss children's (or parents') thoughts and feelings about termination and the difficulties inherent to termination.

In addition, we emphasize once again the progress that has been made in the treatment program and the changes that have occurred in terms of both the children's and parents' behaviors. More importantly, we discuss some of the key features of our program that can be used to help manage other child problem behaviors. For example, parent contingency management and child self-control skills are useful skills that can be used to change other child behaviors. Depending on the particular problem behavior being discussed, we might then give some concrete examples of how these skills can be generalized to help gain control (or modify) other child behaviors.

New and Better Ways

There is always room for new and better ideas and new and better ways of doing things. Successful problem solving has the potential for enlarging and enriching human horizons in ways both large and small. This is clearly the case with respect to helping children in distress.

Up to this point we have shared with you our basic approach for working with children with anxiety and phobic disorders. We have described in concrete, specific detail some of the ideas, concepts, and constructs that we use for organizing our thinking about how to help these children. We have also described in detail some of the procedures and techniques we use in working with these children. We trust that what we have described will be useful to you in your work. However, the essence of being pragmatic is to hold the view that as things change they can (and do) change for the better, but only if we are open to new and better ideas and new and better ways of doing things. This is the essence of the "attitude" that we have defined as pragmatic—the attitude of orientation that is problem solving and contextual.

Consequently, we do not consider the ideas and procedures we have described in this book as things to be mastered and implemented unreflectively. On the contrary, if you find yourself more of a pragmatic therapist than you might have imagined before reading this book, you will understand them to be a starting point rather than an end point. You will understand that the real challenge of the attitude we have described as pragmatic is the challenge of coming up with even better ideas and procedures.

In this, the last part of the book, we share with you some of the ways in which we ourselves have sought to live up to this challenge. We will describe some of the ways in which we have been extending our basic treatment approach to include new and (hopefully) better ideas about treating children in distress. Thus, the concluding part of the book will be more prospective than retrospective. In sharing these ideas with you, we also share with you the way we think about the world—the attitude we bring to all of our efforts—and to challenge or test the limits of the way *you* think about the world and the attitude *you* bring to all of your efforts. Therefore, our goal is to challenge you to be open to the possibility of new and better ideas and procedures and, when they work, to use these in working with the children who come to you for help.

7

Working with Other Problems, Populations, and Contexts

One of the challenges that arise in coming up with new and better ideas and procedures is that of testing the limits of current knowledge and pushing forward the boundaries. Problems that cannot be resolved in the context of existing knowledge challenge or test the limits of that knowledge. Successful problem solving contributes to the process by which knowledge is created and transformed. In this, the final chapter of the book, we turn to the issue of how we have sought to extend our current work to include new and better ways of dealing with the types of problems that often arise in treating children with anxiety and phobic disorders.

TREATING THE CHILD AND PARENT TOGETHER

In this section we describe our efforts in developing an approach for treating the child and parent together that extends our ideas about treatment. What is innovative about this work is that it begins to challenge our assumption about how to work with children with anxiety and phobic disorders. The basic treatment approach that we illustrated in Part III of the book uses a transfer-of-control model for implementing an exposure-based intervention. Recall that this model is based on the premise that treatment effectiveness is maximized by the use of clear and direct pathways of transfer of control (in this case, from the therapist to the parent to the child). In many cases, the use of this pathway as suggested by the model makes the most sense, but not in all cases. As we suggested earlier, sometimes a pathway may be blocked.

There are many ways in which the pathway from therapist to parent to child may be blocked. One way this happens is when parents themselves have severe symptoms of anxiety. A second way is when children have a poor relationship with their parents. When either one of these types of blocks occurs, relying on our usual or routine ideas about treating children with anxiety and phobic disorders may not be the most useful. Relying on our usual or routine ideas is exactly what many of us are likely to do, however. For example, most mental health professionals trained in individually oriented traditions usually focus primarily on working with the child, with the problems of the parents being a secondary focus (or not at all). Or, the parents might be referred elsewhere for help with their problems. Individually oriented therapists are not likely to target in a systematic way the parent–child relationship. Similarly, most mental health professionals trained in the family-oriented traditions usually focus primarily on working with the entire family, with the problems of the child and/or the specific parent–child relationship being a secondary focus (or not at all).

Being pragmatic, however, we not only draw on multiple traditions—we are also open to new ideas and ways of doing things, and with coming up with new ideas and ways of doing things when necessary. That is what we did in this case: We came up with a new way for solving the problem of what to do when the therapist-to-parent-to-child pathway is blocked by parent symptoms and/or a problematic parent–child relationship. In this case, our solution to the problem was to extend the basic treatment approach described in Part III of the book to target the parent symptoms and/or target the parent–child relationship. However, we went beyond the usual assumptions about how to work with children with anxiety and phobic disorders by developing a treatment approach in which the child and parent are seen together at the same time by the same therapist—that is, dyadic treatment.

Dyadic Treatment

Hence, one way in which we are beginning to extend our ideas and procedures is by developing an intervention that targets family relational contextual processes, in addition to individual child processes (i.e., cognitive, behavioral, affective), using a dyadic format. As part of this effort, we have developed a dyadic treatment program and have begun to test it out. We plan to conduct a more complete test of the program in a clinical trials study. We are hopeful that this program will be helpful in solving the problem of what to do when the parent-to-child pathway is blocked by relational contextual processes.

Targeting Parent Symptoms

In working with children you may have gotten the impression that there is more than an element of truth in the old saying, "The apple doesn't fall far from the tree." If you have, you are to be commended for your powers of observation! In fact, considerable research evidence has documented that children with anxiety and phobic disorders are likely to have parents who have anxiety and phobic symptomatology themselves. This evidence comes from both "top-down" and "bottom-up" studies (see Klein & Last, 1989; Silverman, Cerny, & Nelles, 1988; Ginsburg, Silverman, & Kurtines, 1995a). Top-down studies are investigations that examine the prevalence of psychopathology in children whose parents have received an anxiety/phobic diagnosis (e.g., Silverman, Cerny, Nelles, & Burke, 1988; Turner, Beidel, & Costello, 1887; Weissman, Leckman, Merikangas, Gammon, & Prusoff, 1984). Bottom-up studies are investigations that examine the prevalence of psychopathology in parents of children who have received an anxiety/phobic diagnosis (e.g., Bernstein & Garfinkel, 1988; Last, Hersen, Kazdin, Orvaschel, & Perrin, 1991; Messer & Beidel, 1994).

Anyone who has worked with children with anxiety and phobic disorders will also have little difficulty in seeing how such parent anxious symptomatology may serve to block the transfer of control. For example, we have found that parents who avoided certain places or objects would frequently be unable to engage in certain activities (e.g., transport the child) necessary for the occurrence of their child's exposure task. We also have worked with cases where the child's exposure task did not take place because the parent avoided the same places or objects as the child—i.e., the child and parent had the same phobia. Parents have a hard time facilitating the occurrence of their child's exposure if they cannot do the exposure themselves! Along these lines, it is not very helpful for a child to see their parent crying or shouting out with fear or with "warnings" to the child (e.g., "Be careful now"; "Don't get too close!") while the child is trying to do an exposure! This, too, we have observed.

In our dyadic treatment approach, treating parent symptomatology involves applying the same key change-producing procedure (i.e., exposure) and facilitative therapeutic strategies—contingency management and contracting, and self-control. For example, in using contingency management and contracting, contracts are written not just to facilitate child exposure, but also to facilitate parent exposure. Hence, if the parent goes to the shopping mall for 20 minutes, the child gives the parent a back rub. As another example, if the child and parent avoid the same types of situations, they can do their exposure tasks together and then share rewarding activities together.

Targeting Parent–Child Relationship

We have found that many parents have adequate parenting or child management skills (e.g., consistent use of reinforcement and extinction, appropriate modeling behavior)—all of which are likely to facilitate the transfer of control. Moreover, if parents do not have adequate parenting or child management skills, we have found that many parents can learn these skills and can use them effectively after going through our basic program.

It is not difficult to see, however, how a maladaptive parent–child relationship might block the transfer of control. Indeed, parent–child relational processes have long been recognized as an important context for the development and/or maintenance of child fearful or anxious behaviors. Parents of anxious/phobic children have been described in the literature, for example, as interacting with their children in ways viewed as "overprotective" and "ambivalent" (e.g., Berg, Nichols, & Pritchard, 1969; Eisenberg, 1958; also see Kearney & Silverman, 1995, for review). In addition, certain parental child management patterns have been found to be associated with child fear and anxious behaviors (e.g., Bush, Melamed, Sheras, & Greenbaum, 1986; Zabin & Melamed, 1980). We have similarly found that certain ways in which parents manage their child's display of fearful or avoidant behavior appear to serve as blocks. The protection trap we talked about earlier provides an example of the types of parental methods we are talking about. We have worked with scores of parents who use other types of inadequate or inappropriate methods to manage their child's display of fearful or avoidant behavior, such as punishment, physical force, or shame. Methods such as these are likely to render the pathway from parent to child problematic for the transfer of control.

Other aspects of the parent–child relationship that we have found to be blocks are parent–child communication and problem-solving skills. Research findings also indicate that these are problem areas for families of children with anxiety disorders (e.g., Barrett, Rapee, Dadds, & Ryan, 1995; Bernstein & Garfinkel, 1988). Poor parent–child communication, for example, makes it difficult for the child to convey the need for help when a problem arises in the future. In addition, when the child encounters a difficult situation and seeks help from the parent to handle it, if the child and parent lack adequate problem-solving skills, this too may prevent successful resolution of the problem.

Additional Change Producing Procedures

Treating problematic parent–child relationships involved extending our basic treatment approach to include an additional change-producing procedure that targets relational contextual processes. The primary change-producing procedure we use for targeting parent–child relationships is "relationship enhancement skills training." We developed and/or adapted a variety of training strategies that target specific skills enhancing the quality of the parent–child relationship in three domains: (1) advanced child anxiety management skills training; (2) parent-child communication skills training; and (3) parent–child problem-solving skills training. In targeting these particular relationship enhancement skills we specifically focus on maladaptive parent–child interactional patterns that have been implicated in childhood anxiety and that may "block" or impede the transfer of control from parent to child.

Advanced Child Anxiety Management Parent Training

In this training emphasis is placed on training parents in managing their child's anxious behaviors. In addition to training parents in the use of appropriate contingencies to facilitate their child's exposure or approach behavior, emphasis is placed on specific strategies parents can use in order to serve as positive change agents for their child. This includes teaching parents in the use of appropriate types of instructions as well as training in how to serve as a positive coping model. So, for example, we would explain to parents that just as it is not adaptive to show extreme terror or loss of control in front of their child, so it is not adaptive to hide one's feelings of fear or anxiety and pretend that they do not exist. We then talk about a positive coping model as one who may have feelings of fear or anxiety but handles these feelings appropriately (using some of the strategies talked about in the program such as the cognitive strategies) and manages or copes with those feelings. We would role-play with the parent in how to go about displaying positive coping behaviors and provide instructions and feedback.

Parent–Child Communication Training

In this training emphasis is placed on training parents and children in effective communication skills. A key element is learning to listen and respond in nonthreatening ways and identifying more appropriate ways of expressing needs, wants, and emotions. We would also explain to the parents and children the importance of structuring time for daily discussions, and we would practice such discussions during the treatment sessions and provide instructions and feedback to the dyad.

Parent–Child Problem-Solving Training

In this training emphasis is placed on training parents and children in effective problem-solving skills. A key element is training both parent and child in specific problem-solving skills such as mutually identifying the problem, brainstorming a list of possible solutions, selecting a solution, and assessing the solution outcome (D'Zurilla & Goldfried, 1971). The emphasis, in other words, is on working as a team in solving problems. In addition, special emphasis is given to training in how to resolve conflict as it relates to the child's anxiety. Parents, for example, are trained in how to de-escalate conflicts and in better managing children's emotional upsets and noncompliance that may be functionally related to anxiety.

TREATING CHILDREN IN GROUPS

The preceding section covered ideas about how to unblock the pathway from therapist to parent to child. However, sometimes parents are unavailable or unable to commit to treatment and, therefore, it is not possible to work with parent symptoms and/or problematic parent–child relationships. Being pragmatic, we were willing to look beyond our usual way of doing things. In the case of looking for additional pathways, our efforts involved drawing on additional treatment traditions. The treatment approach that emerged out of these efforts draws on the "group" tradition in psychotherapy, and the additional pathways we make use of are those provided by peers. In extending our basic approach to include peers we were also able to solve other types of problems that often arise in treatment. For example, with growing concerns about managed care and accountability, we are all under pressure to identify and use more cost-effective treatments. One way to do this was to extend our basic treatment approach for use in yet another type of format—a group format.

Group Treatment

Hence, a second way that we are beginning to extend our ideas and procedures is by developing an intervention that draws on the group tradition in psychotherapy and that uses peers as a pathway to facilitate the transfer of control. As part of this effort, we have developed a group treatment program and have begun to test it out. We are in the process of conducting a federally funded clinical trials study experimentally testing the effectiveness of the intervention (see Ginsburg, Silverman, & Kurtines, 1995b, for further details).

Targeting Children with Different Diagnoses in the Same Group

In developing our group treatment we wanted the approach to be flexible enough that it could be used with both homogeneous and heterogeneous diagnostic groups. We did not, however, target child problems at random. Because some DSM diagnostic subcategories share common core content, we examined the content of the various diagnostic categories and identified categories that have common content.[1] We then used this common content to develop an approach that could be used with children who would be most likely to be helped by working with their peers in a group. In the case of the group treatment approach we are using in our clinical trials study, we developed a group treatment

---

[1] See the discussion of the relationship between diagnosis and treatment in Chapter 4.

program for heterogeneous diagnoses that includes children diagnosed with Generalized Anxiety Disorder and Social Phobia (Social Anxiety Disorder). Children with these diagnoses share a core content, namely, excessive concern about social evaluation and performance. Given this core content, we designed the approach so that the key change-producing procedure—exposure—centers on a common content, namely, situations that involve social evaluation and performance. Targeting a common core of content also enabled us to include other adjunctive treatment strategies that might be needed such as, in this case, social skills training.

The use of a group format with these children also helped to solve another problem frequently encountered in using exposure-based interventions with children with Social Phobia and Generalized Anxiety Disorder, namely, the difficulty in getting the children to carry out their exposure tasks—tasks involving exposures to social evaluation contexts. Treating children who share a concern about social evaluation and performance together in a group increases the likelihood of their exposure to social evaluation contexts beyond those that are assigned as out-of-session tasks because such exposure is already intrinsic to the group format itself.

Advantages of Working with Group Processes

There are a number of advantages to working with groups. The group format provides the therapist with more extensive and direct access to "natural" processes that can facilitate treatment than in the individual approach. These processes include peer modeling, peer reinforcement and support, and social comparison. For example, when a child in the group observes a peer perform a successful exposure task, it provides the opportunity for positive modeling to occur. The child's subsequent successful completion of his or her own exposure task, in turn, results in peer reinforcement for the child. The group format also provides a context for corrective or instructive feedback (e.g., when children share with each other their methods for doing exposure tasks). In addition, the group process itself provides support for the children. When the children discuss their successful between session experiences, the sharing of these experiences provides positive support for progress. Finally, increasing positive interactions among children in the group contributes to the experience of cohesion and mutual support.

There are several ways in which we draw on these processes. For example, in our group work, we highlight similarities and differences among the group members. We point out how all the children are in this group because most of them are experiencing similar types of feelings and thoughts, or are showing similar types of behaviors. The children are then encouraged to elaborate on this point. We also ask the children to pinpoint some differences in these feelings, thoughts, and behaviors. In addition, at all times, we encourage dialogue among the group members by reminding the children not to talk to us or to ask us questions, but rather to talk to each other and ask each other questions. We also structure exercises that require the children to work together (e.g., working in dyads). This serves to foster trust among the group members and establishes a sense of working together for a common goal.

Practically, treating children with anxiety and phobic disorders in groups offers several advantages. First, it enhances cost-effectiveness in that it makes more efficient use of the therapist's time. Second, it is more cost-effective for children and families because treatment is provided to many children at the same time. Third, group treatment has the potential for making treatment available to children and families for whom it might otherwise not be available.

Additional Treatment Strategies

In addition to the use of group processes, we have included social skills training as an adjunctive treatment strategy. Social skills training is also included because children with diagnoses of Generalized Anxiety Disorder and Social Phobia share a common core content, namely, excessive concern about social evaluation and performance, and also appear to share a common behavioral deficit or difficulty. That is, these children are often either lacking in adequate social skills or they show problematic social skills.

Social Skills Training

In teaching children social skills we make use of such methods as modeling, coaching, and behavioral rehearsal. Specifically, based on in-session rehearsals and role-plays, we target two specific skills for each individual child. We first describe the various skills that exist (e.g., smiling/laughing, greeting others, joining activities, extending invitations, conversational skills, verbal complimenting, and physical appearance/grooming), give appropriate and inappropriate examples of each, and then model each skill for the group (e.g., La Greca & Fetter, 1995). Each child in the group then selects two specific skills that he or she feels would be most helpful to learn. The children then practice the skills with one another in session by role-playing different situations, based on anxiety-provoking social interactions indicated on their daily diaries. Throughout the social skills part of the program, the children receive coaching and feedback from the therapist and other group members.

In addition, we expect the children to engage in practice of these skills outside of the treatment sessions. These out-of-session tasks may involve having the children apply their newly acquired social skills in "real" situations such as initiating a conversation with a peer or asking a peer for his or her phone number. We also ask that the parents assist the children by role-playing these skills at home and monitoring the children's social-exposure exercises.

Now that we have provided an overview of our group treatment approach, we illustrate how the group can be useful for helping children with Generalized Anxiety Disorder and Social Phobia. The case examples described below were drawn from children who participated in our study testing the effectiveness of the group treatment approach.

THE CASE OF MARY, JIMMY, LUCY, AND SAL

Description and History

Mary, a nine-year-old girl, was referred to treatment because her mother felt that her daughter "worried about everything." Some of the things that Mary reportedly worried most about included what others thought of her, whether she was performing well enough in school, and "terrorism." Mother reported that "even little things" made Mary worry, and she needed constant reassurance about "everything." For example, even before coming to her appointment to see us, the mother needed to reassure Mary that "the doctor was not going to give her a shot." Mary's constant worrying also frequently led to many physical complaints, especially severe headaches.

Jimmy, a eight-year-old boy, was referred to treatment because his mother felt her son was "overly sensitive." For example, if she was late in picking him up from the aftercare program in school, Jimmy would get very upset and worry that his mother was not coming and did not love him. In general, Jimmy felt that "no one" really loved him, and he was constantly worrying about what others thought about him. At night, for example, he would frequently cry and be upset about things that other kids said to him that day in school. Jimmy also could not ever be left alone, and because he was afraid of the dark, he slept with his parents in their bed at night.

Lucy, a nine-year-old girl, was referred to treatment by the school counselor. The school counselor felt that Lucy was "too isolated" in school. Specifically, Lucy did not talk to any of the other children in school, she had no friends, and she believed that no one liked her. She was extremely preoccupied with what others thought of her and felt very nervous when she had to be with other people. Because of Lucy's anxiety in social situations, she never went to parties or any other type of social event. Lucy and her mother both acknowledged that Lucy's anxieties and fears were negatively affecting her ability to develop any friend-ships and that Lucy was becoming increasingly distressed about this.

Sal, a 10-year-old boy, was referred to treatment because of his numerous worries about natural disasters, personal safety, and "making God angry." Sal was also protesting more and more each morning about going to school because he worried about what might happen there. Sal felt that he was "not good enough" in his school performance, though he received all As and Bs, but yet he worried about "making mistakes."

Synopsis of Therapy Sessions

Below is a portion of the dialogue occurring during the initial session in which the therapist helps the group members see that they are not alone and that they share similar problems.

T: What are some of the things that make you feel scared or worried?

Jimmy: I worry about being left alone. It scares me when no one is with me because anything can happen. I'm also afraid of the dark.

Sal: I saw on the news these big holes underneath the ground that fill up with water and the ground crumbles in little by little. It scares me that we might be living on ground that might cave in and our house will sink into the ground.

Mary: What others think about me and that I am going to fail math. That is what bothers me.

Sal: Math? I'm pretty good in math, but social studies, science, and reading, forget about it.

T: Lucy, what about you?

Lucy: What?

Sal: Why are you coming here? Are you also failing math?

Lucy: No.

Mary: So how come you are here?

Lucy: I don't know. I guess because I have to make friends. I don't have too many.

Mary: Yeah, me too. I'm scared of getting teased and not having any friends to play with. I'm also afraid of shots.

Jimmy: Kids tease me too. I especially hate it if I have to eat in the cafeteria.

T: So it sounds like all of you have lots of things in common, don't you? Can someone summarize for me what some of these things are?

After obtaining a summary of the commonalities among the children, the therapist would also ask for a summary of the differences.

Next is a portion of the dialogue in which the children in the group share their experiences in carrying out the previous week's exposure task. Part of this dialogue focuses on the children's sharing some of the ideas they learned from the social skills training component of the treatment.

T: Let's remind each other what each of us was supposed to do during this past week in terms of each of our steps on our hierarchies. Let's talk about our exposure task and how it went.

Jimmy: I had to have my mother pick me up only at 5:30 at aftercare, and I couldn't ask the teacher if I could call my mother at work, and then I couldn't cry or complain about it to my mother once she picked me up. My mother took me to the Discovery Zone because I did it.

Group: Awesome!! (all applaud)

Mary: I had to go up to a house by myself and ask if they wanted to buy Girl Scout cookies. I did that while my mom stayed in the car. My reward was that I was able to rent a video.

Group: Yeah!! (all applaud)

T: And Sal, what about you? How did your exposure go this week?

Sal: I had to go to school in the morning, and I couldn't make any fuss at all. I just had to get up, eat breakfast, get washed and dressed, and leave. Boy, I was really scared because it was on Friday and we have spelling tests on Fridays, but I did it. My mother didn't give me the reward yet, but she says she'll give it to me tonight. A Spiderman comic book.

Group: Great job! (all applaud)

Mary: Lucy, what about you?

Lucy: Um, huh, well, I had to ask a kid in my class to play with me during the recess. I didn't do it.

Mary: How come you didn't do it?

Lucy: Because I know no one in my class likes me. No one would want to play with me and then I would feel bad.

Mary: If there are kids you don't know and you want to play with them, you could walk up to them and show them a game.

Jimmy: Yeah, you can go up to them and start talking about a subject until it leads to another subject and it will keep going on and on.

Sal: You can talk to them just like you talk to us. I'll practice with you what to say. First, you ask me a question.

Next is a portion of the dialogue in which the children in the group practice using their self-control skills. In particular, the children practice together modifying their anxious thoughts with more adaptive coping thoughts and behaviors. They also practice evaluating their skills in controlling their anxious thoughts and praising themselves for doing so.

T: Let's practice "O" —changing our scary thoughts to *other* coping thoughts and actions that will help you handle the situation.

Jimmy: First when I think that my mother might not pick me up and instead some crazy people out there will come and kidnap me, I think about how the school carefully checks who each kid goes home with, so what's the chance that a kidnapper would be able to come into my school and kidnap me? It's never happened before.

Mary: My scary thought is I'll fall in the pool and die but my "O" is, "it's a million to one that I'll fall in the pool and even if I do my mom is right there to help me."

Sal: I think I am going to make all these mistakes in school and all the kids are going to think I'm a dork, so I don't like to go to school. But my "O" is I do pretty good in school and even if I do make a mistake I won't die and school is fun too sometimes.

Lucy: But I don't like it when people laugh at me. Then everyone will laugh at me and I want to leave school.

Mary (to Lucy): So what if they tease you, they can't murder you or anything!

Sal (to Lucy): If they tease you, just ignore it.

Mary (to Lucy): Just don't think about what they say.

T: Well, Lucy, it sounds like you are getting some really good ideas from everyone. What do you think?

Lucy: I guess I'll try it. I have nothing to lose if I try it at least.

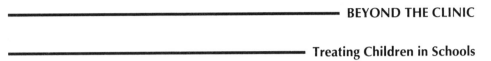

BEYOND THE CLINIC

Treating Children in Schools

Up to this point our focus has been on treatment approaches for helping children with diagnosable anxiety and phobic disorders in clinic settings. Mental health professionals, however, are frequently called upon to help children in other types of contexts. In trying to help, issues may arise that challenge mental health professionals to go beyond their ordinary or routine ways of doing things. As we have suggested, this is where being pragmatic is especially useful. The treatment approach we describe in this section illustrates how one can begin with a concrete, specific problem that human beings experience, and use this as a starting point in challenging the limits of existing ideas and procedures. In this case, the problem was what to do about helping the growing number of children who are exposed to crime and violence.

Interestingly enough, although we are all increasingly aware of the impact that the growth of crime and violence has had on our country's youth, it was a specific event involving a particular girl that crystallized our efforts to develop a treatment approach for helping these youth. Specifically, one morning the center staff were discussing some very dramatic news footage that had been shown on the evening news. It turned out that we had all seen it on television the night before. The video portion depicted the scene of a particularly gruesome murder/suicide. A single mother and her 13-year-old daughter had rented a room in their trailer to a man who, in a subsequent rage, left the trailer and returned with a gun. When the boarder returned, he shot and killed the mother. At the time of the shooting, the daughter hid under the bed with a telephone. The man then barricaded himself in the trailer when the SWAT team arrived and, meanwhile, the young girl remained hidden under the bed. For the next several hours, she remained hidden under the bed, in continuous contact with the 911 operator. The audio portion of the newscast reported "live" the recorded, desperate voice of the child, including her pleas for help, her description of the man's activities, and observations of her dead mother on the floor. By the time the SWAT team stormed the trailer later in the evening, the man was found dead from an apparent suicide.

In discussing this event at the center, the issue arose of the profound effect that witnessing such an event must have on the child as well as what could be done to help her. This issue also arose in a subsequent discussion we had with one of our colleagues who happened to be an administrator at the school this child attended. Our colleague further commented to us that although this particular incident was out of the range of ordinary experience, many of the students in his school are routinely exposed to traumatic events involving crime and violence. He further informed us that there were no programs that specifically targeted this particular problem.

At this point we discussed whether the types of clinic-based programs that we were running in our center could be extended beyond the clinic. Being pragmatic, we realized that if we really wanted to do something useful for this particular problem (i.e., help youth who had been exposed to crime and violence), we needed to move beyond our routine or ordinary ways of doing things; we needed to get out of the clinic and take the intervention to where it would do the most good. In particular, inner-city youth who are most likely to be chronically exposed to crime and violence are not likely to be seen for treatment in mental health clinics. We therefore had to take the intervention to these youth because crime and violence have become so much a part of the culture of modern American life that exposure to such traumatic events among many youth has become the norm. Such youth are, consequently, unlikely to recognize the effects of this exposure (e.g., anxiety-related symptoms, such as those of Posttraumatic Stress Disorder [PTSD]) as "problems" in need of mental health services. We needed to develop a time- and cost-effective intervention that could be adopted for use in diverse community-based settings (e.g., schools, juvenile courts) by institution-based practitioners (e.g., school counselors, social workers). We needed to develop an intervention that could be implemented in the contexts and settings where it would do the most good.

In trying to help, we were once again challenged to go beyond the limits of our existing ideas and ways of doing things. In this case, our solution to the problem was to extend the group treatment approach that we have been testing in a clinic setting for use in institutional settings with youth who have been exposed to crime and violence in a school-based setting.

School-Based Treatment

Hence, a third way that we are beginning to extend our ideas about treatment is by developing an intervention that goes beyond the clinic to make mental health services available to a population that is otherwise unlikely to receive it, namely, a multiethnic population of urban youth who have been exposed to crime or violence, as either a victim or witness. The school-based intervention that we developed uses the same key change-producing procedure—exposure—as our basic individual and group treatment approaches. However, the treatment program for our school-based intervention also draws on our group approach. Because parents are not readily available in school-based contexts to facilitate the transfer of control, we needed an approach that made use of peers to facilitate the transfer. The group approach is also a time- and cost-effective approach, and its many practical advantages facilitate its use in institutional settings.

Targeting PTSD Symptomatology

In extending our basic approach for use in a school-based setting our goal was to develop an intervention for use with youth who are exposed to crime and violence. Although reactions to exposure to crime and violence are complex and multifaceted, there is growing evidence that distress symptoms of the type associated with posttraumatic stress is a primary consequence of such exposure. More specifically, research with high-risk urban youth (Berman, Kurtines, Silverman, & Ramos, 1995; Richters & Martinez, 1993) has suggested that symptoms associated with posttraumatic stress constitute a central feature of the distress reaction that youth exhibit when exposed to crime and violence. Although many youth who are exposed to crime and violence do not exhibit distress symptoms severe enough either in intensity or duration to meet criteria for a diagnosis of PTSD, the emerging evidence indicates that most will have some level of posttraumatic stress symptoms. Because urban youth are at a high risk for exposure to crime and violence, we developed the intervention for use with youth who have experienced varying degrees of exposure and varying levels of symptoms—*not* simply those who meet diagnostic criteria for PTSD.

Additional Treatment Strategies

Our school-based intervention for youth exposed to crime and violence also draws on growing evidence that coping response and social support buffer stressful life events. In developing our intervention we designed it to target the victim/witness's capacity to generate adaptive coping responses and to access and utilize social support as a potential buffer of exposure to crime and violence and/or symptoms associated with traumatic events. Consequently, we have also included treatment strategies that focus on coping skills enhancement and social support enhancement.

Enhancing the Use of Adaptive Coping Responses. Exposure to crime and violence challenges the victim/witness's capacity to generate adaptive coping response and promotes the use of maladaptive coping responses. These might include self-blame, anger, withdrawal, blaming others, and so on. Moreover, these maladaptive coping responses, if sufficiently intense, may facilitate the intrusive memories and avoidance reactions associated with posttraumatic stress, and interfere with successful emotional processing during the exposure-based exercise. The coping skills enhancement training used in our school-based intervention provides the youth with corrective information as it relates to a particular maladaptive coping response. Coping skills enhancement thus not only improves the coping responses of the youth, but also serves to moderate the reduction of posttraumatic stress symptoms. The cognitive coping techniques are taught using the same strategies (i.e., the STOP model) that we use in our basic treatment approach.

Enhancing Social Support Availability and Utilization. Peers serve as a major source of social support for youth (Levitt, 1991), and traumatic events deplete social support (Kaniasty & Norris, 1993). Existing evidence suggests that the broader and deeper the network of social support, the greater the chance of ameliorating the negative effects of stressful life events. One focus of the social support enhancement training is on the group itself as a source of social support. In addition, based on our preliminary findings and the work of others (see Keppel-Benson & Ollendick, 1993), we also make an active effort to enhance external sources of social support. In this effort, we make a distinction between perceived and received support and consistent with the conceptualization of Kaniasty and Norris (1992), we make an active effort to enhance both aspects. Specifically, in helping youth to identify support agents, we point out that they have "more support than they think they have" (perceived support), and we teach the youth how to engage outside sources (e.g., parents, siblings, friends) as support agents (received support). To help accomplish this, behavioral techniques such as contingency contracting, modeling, role-playing, and feedback are used.

Role of Group Process. The group format is especially useful for working with youth who have been a witness or victim of crime and violence (Alessi & Hearn, 1984). Group processes can facilitate the discussion of content related to the traumatic event. For example, within the group, discussions of the youth's reactions are normalized and universalized. A group format is also consistent with the fact that symptoms associated with posttraumatic stress often result from traumatic events that expose groups of individuals to crime or violence in public places (e.g., shootings in schools, stores, or restaurants; snipers; hostage taking).

However, even when individuals do not experience exactly the same traumatic event, in cases such as exposure to crime and violence, individuals experience very similar events. The group format provides a natural setting for these individuals to address their shared experience and seek support with others experiencing similar effects.

Layering. In using our group approach in a school-based intervention, we have also extended the transfer-of-control model to include the concept of "layering." The phases of the intervention involve the sequential implementation in "layers" of the exposure tasks via our basic cognitive and behavioral facilitative strategies and supplemented with the additional treatment strategies. For example, in implementing our treatment program, the exposure exercises begin in session 3. Session 4 begins the "layering" process by initiating the group-based coping skills enhancement training. Session 5 continues the layering process by initiating the group-based social-support enhancement training. This type of layering process is extended throughout the 12-week program.

In summary, our efforts to help youth who have been exposed to crime and violence began with the problems of a concrete, specific human being. The experiences of the young girl trapped in a nightmare served as our starting point. Her experiences challenged our ideas about treatment and ways of doing therapy. In taking up the challenge we had to move beyond helping children with diagnosable disorders to youth with a full range of symptoms, beyond a clinic setting to the community, and beyond interventions that target symptoms to interventions that enhance positive functioning. The goal of our school-based intervention is to help youth exposed to crime and violence by reducing their posttraumatic stress symptoms, by enhancing their use of adaptive coping responses, and by enhancing their effective use of available social support. Coming up with ways for solving human problems has the potential for enlarging and enriching human horizons in ways both large and small, and for helping young people in distress in no small way.

EPILOGUE

As pragmatic therapists our view is that "studying people involves refining understanding, not achieving final proof" (Glassie, 1982). Hence, the best way "to find out what to believe is to listen to as many suggestions and arguments as you can" (Rorty, 1989). It was this view that inspired us to share with you some of our ideas about treatment and our ways of doing therapy. Consequently, although we would consider the effort we put into this book worthwhile if the treatment approach we have outlined proves useful in your work, we are grateful as well for your reading of the book, and thus, your listening to us. We thank you simply for that.

References

Abe, K. (1972). Phobias and nervous symptoms in childhood and maturity: Persistence and associations. *British Journal of Psychiatry, 120*, 275–283.

Achenbach, T. M., & Edelbrock, C. (1991). *Manual for the child behavior checklist and revised child behavior profile* (Rev.). Burlington: Department of Psychiatry, University of Vermont.

Alessi, J. J., & Hearn, K. (1984). Group treatment of children in shelters for battered women. In A. R. Roberts (Ed.), *Battered women and their families: Intervention strategies and treatment programs* (pp. 49–61). New York: Springer.

Ambrosini, P. J., Metz, C., Prabucki, K., & Lee, J. C. (1989). Videotape reliability of the third revised edition of the K-SADS. *Journal of the American Academy of Child and Adolescent Psychiatry, 28*, 723–728.

American Psychiatric Association. (1980). *Diagnostic and statistical manual of mental disorders* (3rd ed.). Washington, DC: Author.

American Psychiatric Association. (1987). *Diagnostic and statistical manual of mental disorders* (3rd ed. Rev.). Washington, DC: Author.

American Psychiatric Association. (1994). *Diagnostic and statistical manual of mental disorders* (4th ed.). Washington, DC: Author.

Angold, A., & Costello, E. J. A test-retest reliability study of child-reported psychiatric symptoms and disgnoses using the Child and Adolescent Psychiatric Assessment (CAPA-C). *Psychological Medicine*, in press.

Atkinson, L., Quarrington, B., Cyr, J. J., & Atkinson, F. V. (1989). Differential classification in school refusal. *British Journal of Psychiatry, 155*, 191–195.

Barlow, D. H. (1988). *Anxiety and its disorders: The nature and treatment of anxiety and panic*. New York: Guilford Press.

Barrett, P. M., Rapee, R. M., Dadds, M. M., & Ryan, S. M. *Family enhancement of cognitive style in anxious and aggressive children: Threat bias and the FEAR effect*, submitted for publication.

Beck, A. T., & Emery, G. (1985). *Anxiety disorders and phobias: A cognitive perspective*. New York: Basic Books.

Beidel, D. C., Neal, A. M., & Lederer, A. S. (1991). The feasibility and validity of a daily diary for the assessment of anxiety in children. *Behavior Therapy, 22*, 505–517.

Beidel, D. C., Turner, S. M., & Morris, T. L. (1995). A new inventory to assess childhood social anxiety and phobia: The Social Phobia Anxiety Inventory for Children. *Psychological Assessment, 7*, 73–79.

Berg, I., Nichols, K., & Pritchard, C. (1969). School-phobia—its classification and relationship to dependency. *Journal of Child Psychology and Psychiatry, 10*, 123–141.

Berman, S. L., Kurtines, W. M., Silverman, W. K., & Ramos, L. (1995). The impact of exposure to crime and violence on urban youth, submitted for publication.

Bernstein, G. A., & Garfinkel, B. D. (1988). Pedigrees, functioning, and psychopathology in families of school phobic children. *Journal of the American Academy of Child and Adolescent Psychiatry, 27,* 70–74.

Burke, A. E., & Silverman, W. K. (1987). The prescriptive treatment of school refusal. *Clinical Psychology Review, 7,* 353–362.

Bush, J. P., Melamed, B. G., Sheras, P. L., & Greenbaum, P. E. (1986). Mother-child patterns of coping with anticipatory medical stress. *Health Psychology, 5,* 137–157.

Chambers, W. J., Puig-Antich, J., Hirsch, M., Paez, P., Ambrosini, P. J., Tabrizi, M. S., & Davies, M. (1985). The assessment of affective disorders in children and adolescents by semistructured interview. *Archives of General Psychiatry, 42,* 696–702.

Cohen, P., O'Connor, P., Lewis, S., Velez, N., & Malachowski, B. (1987). Comparison of DISC and K-SADS-P interviews of an epidemiological sample of children. *Journal of the American Academy of Child and Adolescent Psychiatry, 26,* 662–667.

Costello, A. J., Edelbrock, C. S., Dulcan, M. K., Kalas, R., & Klaric, S. H. (1984). *Report to NIMH on the NIMH diagnostic interview schedule for children (DISC).* Washington, DC: National Institute of Mental Health.

Costello, E. J., & Angold, A. (1988). Scales to assess child and adolescent depression: Checklists, screens, and nets. *Journal of the American Academy of Child and Adolescent Psychiatry, 27,* 726–737.

D'Zurilla, T. J., & Goldfried, M. R. (1971). Problem solving and behavior modification. *Journal of Abnormal Psychology, 78,* 107–126.

Dewey, J. (1920). *Reconstruction in philosophy.* New York: Henry Holt & Co.

Dewey, J. (1922). *Human nature and conduct.* New York: Henry Holt & Co.

Di Nardo, P. A., O'Brien, G. T., Barlow, D. H., Waddell, M. T., & Blanchard, E. B. (1983). Reliability of DSM-III anxiety disorder categories using a new structured interview. *Archives of General Psychiatry, 40,* 1070–1079.

Edelbrock, C., & Costello, A. (1984). Structured psychiatric interviews for children and adolescents. In G. Goldstein & M. Hersen (Eds.), *Handbook of psychological assessment,* (pp. 276–290). New York: Pergamon Press.

Edelbrock, C., Costello, A. J., Dulcan, M. K., Kalas, R., & Conover, N. C. (1985). Age differences in the reliability of the psychiatric interview of the child. *Child Development, 56,* 265–275.

Eisenberg, L. (1958). School phobia: Diagnosis, genesis and clinical management. *Pediatric Clinics of North America, 5,* 645–666.

Finch, A. J., Jr., Lipovsky, J. A., & Casat, C. D. (1989). Anxiety and depression in children and adolescents: Negative affectivity or separate constructs? In P. C. Kendall & D. Watson (Eds.), *Anxiety and depression: Distinctive and overlapping features* (pp. 171–196). San Diego: Academic Press.

Finch, A. J., Saylor, C. F., Edwards, G. L., & McIntosh, J. A. (1987). Children's depression inventory: Reliability over repeated administrations. *Journal of Clinical Child Psychology, 16,* 339–341.

Foa, E. B., & Kozak, M. J. (1986). Emotional processing of fear: Exposure to corrective information. *Psychological Bulletin, 99,* 20–35.

Francis, G., Last, C. G., & Strauss, C. C. (1987). Expression of separation anxiety disorder: The roles of age and gender. *Child Psychiatry and Human Development, 18,* 82–89.

Ginsburg, G. S., Silverman, W. K., & Kurtines, W. M. (1995a). Family involvement in treating children with phobic and anxiety disorders: A look ahead. *Clinical Psychology Review. 15*, 457–473.

Ginsburg, G. S., Silverman, W. K., & Kurtines, W. M. (1995b). Cognitive-behavioral group therapy. In A. R. Eisen, C. A. Kearney, & C. E. Schaefer (Eds.), *Clinical handbook of anxiety disorders in children* (pp. 521–549). Northvale, NJ: Jason Aronson.

Glassie, H. (1982). *Passing the time in Ballymenone: Culture and history of an Ulster community.* Philadephia, PA: University of Pennsylvania Press.

Hammond-Laurence, K., Ginsburg, G. S., & Silverman, W. K. (1994, October). *Comorbidity among childhood anxiety and externalizing disorders.* Paper presented at the meeting of Clinical Child Psychology, University of Kansas, Lawrence.

Hawkins, R. P. (1986). Selection of target behaviors. In R. O. Nelson & S. C. Hayes (Eds.), *Conceptual foundations of behavioral assessment* (pp. 331–385). New York: Guilford Press.

Herjanic, B., Herjanic, M., Brown, F., & Wheatt, T. (1975). Are children reliable reporters? *Journal of Abnormal Child Psychology, 3*, 41–48.

Hobbs, N. (1975). *The futures of children: Categories, labels, and their consequences.* San Francisco: Jossey-Bass.

Hodges, K. (1990). Depression and anxiety in children: A comparison of self-report questionnaires to clinical interview. *Psychological Assessment, 2*, 376–381.

Hodges, K., Cools, J., & McKnew, D. (1989). Test-retest reliability of a clinical research interview for children: The Child Assessment Schedule. *Psychological Assessment, 1*, 317–322.

Institute of Medicine. (1989). *Research on children and adolescents with mental, behavioral, and developmental disorders.* Washington, DC: National Academy Press.

Israel, A. C., Guile, C. A., Baker, J. E., & Silverman, W. K. (1994). An evaluation of enhanced self-regulation training in the treatment of childhood obesity. *Journal of Pediatric Psychology, 19*, 737–749.

Israel, A. C. Stolmaker, L., Sharp, J. P., Silverman, W. K., & Simon, L. G. (1984). An evaluation of two methods of parental involvement in treating obese children. *Behavior Therapy, 15*, 266–272.

Kanfer, F. H., Karoly, P., & Newman, A. (1975). Reduction of children's fear of the dark by confidence-related and situation threat-related verbal cues. *Journal of Consulting and Clinical Psychology, 43*, 251–258.

Kaniasty, K., & Norris, F. (1992). Social support and victims of crime: Matching event, support, and outcome. *American Journal of Community Psychology, 20*, 211–241.

Kaniasty, K., & Norris, F. (1993). A test of the social support deterioration model in the context of natural disaster. *Journal of Personality and Social Psychology, 64*, 395–408.

Kashani, J. H. & Orvaschel, H. (1988). Anxiety disorders in mid-adolescence: A community sample. *American Journal of Psychiatry, 145*, 960–964.

Kazdin, A. E. (1993). Psychotherapy for children and adolescents: Current progress and future research directions. *American Psychologist, 48*, 644–657.

Kearney, C. A., & Silverman, W. K. (1992). Let's not push the "panic button": A cautionary analysis of panic disorder in adolescents. *Clinical Psychology Review, 12*, 293–302.

Kearney, C. A., & Silverman, W. K. (1995). Family environment of youngsters with school refusal behavior: A synopsis with implications for assessment and treatment. *American Journal of Family Therapy, 23*, 59–72.

Kearney, C. A., Eisen, A. R., & Silverman, W. K. (1995). The legend and myth of school phobia. *School Psychology Quarterly, 10,* 65–85.

Kendall, P. C., & Chansky, T. E. (1991). Considering cognition in anxiety-disordered children. *Journal of Anxiety Disorders, 5,* 167–185.

Kendall, P. C., Kane, M., Howard, B., & Siqueland, L. (1990). *Cognitive-behavioral therapy for anxious children: Treatment manual.* Available from the author, 238 Meeting House Lane, Merion, PA 19066.

Kendall, P. C., Kortlander, E., Chansky, T. E., & Brady, E. U. (1992). Comorbidity of anxiety and depression in youth: Treatment implications. *Journal of Consulting and Clinical Psychology, 60,* 869–880.

Keppel-Benson, J. M., & Ollendick, T. H. (1993). Posttraumatic stress disorder in children and adolescents. In C. F. Saylor (Ed.), *Children and disasters* (pp.29–43). New York: Plenum Press.

King, N. J., Gullone, E., Tonge, B. J., & Ollendick, T. H. (1993). Self-reports of panic attacks and manifest anxiety in adolescents. *Behaviour Research and Therapy, 31,* 111–116.

King, N. J. (1980). The therapeutic utility of abbreviated progressive relaxation: A critical review with implications for clinical practice. In M. Hersen, R. E. Eisler, & P. Miller (Eds.), *Progress in behavior modification* (Vol. 10. pp. 147–174). New York: Academic Press.

King, N. J., Ollendick, T. H., & Gullone, E. (1991). Negative affectivity in children and adolescents: Relations between anxiety and depression. *Clinical Psychology Review, 11,* 441–459.

Klein, R. G. (1991). Parent-child agreement in clinical assessment of anxiety and other psychopathology: A review. *Journal of Anxiety Disorders, 5,* 187–198.

Klein, R. G., & Last, C. G. (1989). *Anxiety disorders in children.* Newbury Park, CA: Sage Publications.

Kovacs, M. (1985). The interview schedule for children (ISC). *Psychopharmacology Bulletin, 21,* 991–994.

Kurtines, W. M., & Szapocznik, J. (1996). Family interaction patterns: Structural family therapy in contexts of cultural diversity. In E. D. Hibbs & P. Jensen (Eds.), *Psychosocial treatment of child and adolescent disorders: Empirically based approaches.* Washington, DC: American Psychological Association.

La Greca, A. M. (1990). Issues and perspectives on the child assessment process. In A. M. La Greca (Ed.), *Through the eyes of the child: Obtaining self-reports from children and adolescents* (pp. 3–17). Needham Hts, MA: Allyn and Bacon.

La Greca, A. M., & Fetter, M. D. (1995). Peer relations. In A. R. Eisen, C. A. Kearney, & C. E. Schaefer (Eds.), *Clinical handbook of anxiety disorders in children and adolescents* (pp. 80–130). Northvale, NJ: Jason Aronson.

La Greca, A. M., & Stone, W. L. (1993). The Social Anxiety Scale for Children-Revised: Factor structure and concurrent validity. *Journal of Clinical Child Psychology, 22,* 17–27.

Lang, P. J. (1977). Imagery in therapy: An information processing analysis of fear. *Behavior Therapy, 8,* 862–886.

Last, C. G. (1986). Modification of the K-SADS-P for use with anxiety disordered children and adolescents. Unpublished manuscript.

Last, C. G. (1987). Developmental considerations. In C. G. Last & M. Hersen (Eds.), *Issues in diagnostic research* (pp. 201–216). New York: Plenum Press.

Last, C. G., Hersen, M., Kazdin, A., Orvaschel, H., & Perrin, S. (1991). Anxiety disorders in children and their families. *Archives of General Psychiatry, 48,* 928–934.

Last, C. G., Francis, G., & Strauss, C. C. (1989). Assessing fears in anxiety-disordered children with the revised Fear Survey Schedule for Children (FSSC-R). *Journal of Clinical Child Psychology, 18*, 137.

Last, C. G., Perrin, S., Hersen, M., & Kazdin, A. E. (1992). DSM-III-R anxiety disorders in children: Sociodemographic and clinical characteristics. *Journal of the American Academy of Child and Adolescent Psychiatry, 31*, 1070–1076.

Levitt, M. J. (1991). Attachment and close relationships: A life-span perspective. In J. L.Gewirtz & W. M. Kurtines (Eds.), *Intersections with attachment* (pp. 183–205). Hillsdale, NJ: Lawrence Erlbaum.

Loeber, R., Green, S. M., & Lahey, B. B. (1990). Mental health professionals' perception of the utility of children, mothers, and teachers as informants on childhood psychopathology. *Journal of Clinical Child Psychology, 19*, 136–143.

Lonigan, C. J. Carey, M. P., & Finch, A. J., Jr. (1994). Anxiety and depression in children and adolescents: Negative affectivity and the utility of self-reports. *Journal of Consulting and Clinical Psychology, 62*, 1000–1008.

Lyons, J. A. (1987). Posttraumatic stress disorder in children and adolescents: A review of the literature. *Developmental and Behavioral Pediatrics, 8*, 349–356.

Mattison, R. E., Bagnato, S. J., & Brubaker, B. M. (1988). Diagnostic utility of the revised children's manifest anxiety scale in children with DSM-III anxiety disorders. *Journal of Anxiety Disorders, 2*, 147–155.

McGee, R., Feehan, M. Williams, S., Partridge, F., Silva, P. A., & Kelly, J. (1990). DSM-III disorders in a large sample of adolescents. *Journal of the American Academy of Child and Adolescent Psychiatry, 29*, 611–619.

Messer, S. C., & Beidel, D. C. (1994). Psychosocial correlates of childhood anxiety disorders. *Journal of the American Academy of Child and Adolescent Psychiatry, 33*, 975–983.

Mowrer, O. H. (1960). *Learning theory and the symbolic processes.* New York: John Wiley.

Nelles, W. B., & Barlow, D. H. (1988). Do children panic? *Clinical Psychology Review, 8*, 359–372.

Nelson, W. M. III, & Politano, P. M. (1990). Children's Depression Inventory: Stability over repeated administrations in psychiatric inpatient children. *Journal of Clinical Child Psychology, 19*, 254–256.

Norvell, N., Brophy, C., & Finch, A. J. (1985). The relationship of anxiety to childhood depression. *Journal of Personality Assessment, 49*, 150–153.

Ollendick, T. H. (1983). Reliability and validity of the revised Fear Survey Schedule for Children (FSSC-R). *Behaviour Research and Therapy, 21*, 395–399.

Ollendick, T. H., Mattis, S. G., & King, N. J. (1994). Panic in children and adolescents: A review. *Journal of Child Psychology and Psychiatry, 32*, 113–134.

Ost, L. (1987). Age of onset in different phobias. *Journal of Abnormal Psychology, 96*, 123–145.

Perrin, S., & Last, C. G. (1992). Do childhood anxiety measures measure anxiety. *Journal of Abnormal Child Psychology, 20*, 567–578.

Piacentini, J. C., Cohen, P., & Cohen, J. (1992). Combining discrepant diagnostic information from multiple sources: Are complex algorithms better than simple ones? *Journal of Abnormal Child Psychology, 20*, 51–63.

Rabian, B., Ginsburg, G., & Silverman, W. K. (1994). ADIS-R for children. In J. S. March (Chair), *New developments in assessing child and adolescent anxiety disorders.* Symposium conducted at the meeting of the Anxiety Disorders Association of America, Santa Monica, CA; March, 1994.

Rapee, R. M., Barrett, P. M., Dadds, M. R., & Evans, L. (1994). Reliability of the DSM-III-R childhood anxiety disorders using structured interview: Interrater and parent–child agreement. *Journal of the American Academy of Child and Adolescent Psychiatry, 33*, 984–992.

Reynolds, C. R., & Richmond, B. O. (1978). What I think and feel: A revised measure of children's manifest anxiety. *Journal of Abnormal Child Psychology, 6*, 271–280.

Reynolds, C. R., & Richmond, B. O. (1985). *Revised Children's Manifest Anxiety Scale*. Los Angeles: Western Psychological Services.

Richardson, S. A., Dohrenwend, B. S., & Klein, D. (1965). *Interviewing: Its forms and functions*. New York: Basic Books.

Richters, J., & Martinez, P. (1993). The NIMH community violence project: I. Children as victims of and witnesses to violence. *Psychiatry, 56*, 7–21.

Rorty, R. (1979). *Philosophy and the mirror of nature*. Princeton, NJ: Princeton University Press.

Rorty, R. (1985). Solidarity or objectivity? In J. Rajchman & C. West (Eds.), *Post-analytic philosophy* (pp. 3–19). New York: Columbia University Press.

Rorty, R. (1989). *Contingency, irony, and solidarity*. New York: Cambridge University Press.

Rorty, R. (1992). *Consequences of pragmatism: Essays 1972–1980*. Minneapolis: University of Minnesota Press.

Sarason, S., Davidson, K., Lighthall, F., & Waite, R. (1958). A test anxiety scale for children. *Child Development, 29*, 105–113.

Saylor, C. F. (Ed.). (1993). *Children and disasters*. New York: Plenum Press.

Saylor, C. F., Finch, A. J., Jr., Spirito, A., & Bennett, B. (1984). The Children's Depression Inventory: A systematic evaluation of psychometric properties. *Journal of Consulting and Clinical Psychology, 52*, 955–967.

Schwab-Stone, M., Fisher, P., Piacentini, J., Shaffer, D., Davies, M., & Briggs, M. (1993). The Diagnostic Interview Schedule for Children–Revised version (DISC-R). II. Test–retest reliability. *Journal of the American Academy of Child and Adolescent Psychiatry, 32*, 651–657.

Silverman, W. K. (1991). Diagnostic reliability of anxiety disorders in children using structured interviews. *Journal of Anxiety Disorders, 5*, 105–124.

Silverman, W. K. (1994). Structured diagnostic interviews. In T. H. Ollendick, N. King, & W. Yule (Eds.), *International handbook of phobic and anxiety disorders in children and adolescents* (pp. 293–315). New York: Plenum Press.

Silverman, W. K., & Eisen, A. R. (1992). Age differences in the reliability of parent and child reports of child anxious symptomatology using a structured interview. *Journal of American Academy of Child and Adolescent Psychiatry, 31*, 117–124.

Silverman, W. K., & Kurtines, W. M. (1996). Transfer of control: A psychosocial intervention model for disorders in youth. In E. D. Hibbs & P. Jensen (Eds.), *Psychosocial treatment of child and adolescent disorders: Empirically based approaches*. Washington, DC: American Psychological Association.

Silverman, W. K., & Nelles, W. B. (1988). The Anxiety Disorders Interview Schedule for Children. *Journal of the American Academy of Child and Adolescent Psychiatry, 27*, 772–778.

Silverman, W. K., & Rabian, B. (1995). Test-retest reliability of the DSM-III-R anxiety childhood disorders symptoms using the Anxiety Disorders Interview Schedule for Children. *Journal of Anxiety Disorders, 9*, 1–12.

Silverman, W. K., Cerny, J. A., & Nelles, W. B. (1988). The familial influence in anxiety disorders: Studies on the offspring of patients with anxiety disorders. In B. B. Lahey & A. E. Kazdin (Eds.), *Advances in clinical child psychology* (Vol.11, pp. 223–248). New York: Plenum Press.

Silverman, W. K., Cerny, J. A., Nelles, W. B., & Burke, A. E. (1988). Behavior problems in children of parents with anxiety disorders. *Journal of the American Academy of Child and Adolescent Psychiatry, 27,* 779–784.

Silverman, W. K., Fleisig, W., Rabian, B., & Peterson, R. A. (1991). Childhood anxiety sensitivity index. *Journal of Clinical Child Psychology, 20,* 162–168.

Silverman, W. K., Ginsburg, G. S., & Kurtines, W. M. (1995). Clinical issues in the treatment of children with anxiety and phobic disorders. *Cognitive and Behavioral Practice, 2,* 93–117.

Spielberger, C. D. (1973). *Manual for the State-Trait Anxiety Inventory for Children.* Palo Alto, CA: Consulting Psychologists Press.

Spivack, G., & Shure, M. B. (1974). *Social adjustment of young children.* San Francisco: Jossey Bass.

Spivack, G. & Shure, M. B. (1982). Interpersonal cognitive problem solving and clinical theory. In B. Lahey & A. E. Kazdin (Eds.), *Advances in child clinical psychology* (Vol. 5, pp. 323–372). New York: Plenum.

Spivack, G., Platt, J. J., & Shure, M. B. (1976). *The problem solving approach to adjustment.* San Franscisco: Josey Bass.

Terr, L. C. (1991). Childhood traumas—An outline and overview. *American Journal of Psychiatry, 148,* 10–20.

Teyber, E. (1988). *Interpersonal process in psychotherapy: A guide for clinical training.* Illinois: Dorsey Press.

Treiber, F. A., & Mabe, P. A. (1987). Child and parent perceptions of children's psychopathology in psychiatric outpatient children. *Journal of Abnormal Child Psychology, 13,* 115–124.

Turner, S. M., Beidel, D. C., & Costello, A. (1987). Psychopathology in the offspring of anxiety disorders patients. *Journal of Consulting and Clinical Psychology, 55,* 229–235.

Vecchio, T. (1966). Predictive value of a single diagnostic test in unselected populations. *New England Journal of Medicine, 275,* 1171–1173.

Voeltz, L. M., & Evans, I. M. (1982). The assessment of behavioral interrelationships in child behavior therapy. *Behavioral Assessment, 4,* 131–165.

Watson, D., & Clark, L. A. (1984). Negative affectivity: The disposition to experience aversive emotional states. *Psychological Bulletin, 96,* 465–490.

Watson, D., & Kendall, P. C. (1989). Common and differentiating features of anxiety and depression: Current findings and future directions. In P. C. Kendall & D. Watson (Eds.), *Anxiety and depression: Distinctive and overlapping features* (pp. 493–508). San Diego: Academic Press.

Watson, D., Clark, L. A., & Carey, G. (1988). Positive and negative affectivity and their relation to anxiety and depressive disorders. *Journal of Abnormal Psychology, 97,* 346–353.

Weissman, M. M., Leckman, J. F., Merikangas, K. R., Gammon, G. D., & Prusoff, B. A. (1984). Depression and anxiety disorders in parents and children. *Archives of General Psychiatry, 41,* 845–852.

Welner, Z., Reich, W., Herjanic, B., Jung, K. G., & Amado, H. (1987). Reliability, validity, and parent-child agreement studies of the diagnostic interview for children and adolescents (DICA). *Journal of the American Academy of Child and Adolescent Psychiatry, 26,* 649–653.

Whitaker, A., Johnson, J., Shaffer, D., Rapoport, J., Kalikow, K., Walsh, B. T., Davies, M., Braiman, S., & Dolinsky, A. (1990). Uncommon troubles in young people: Prevalence estimates of selected psychiatric disorders in a nonreferred adolescent population. *Archives of General Psychiatry, 47*, 487–496.

Zabin, M. A., & Melamed, B. G. (1980). Relationship between parental discipline and children's ability to cope with stress. *Journal of Behavioral Assessment, 2*, 17–38.

Zoccolillo, M. (1992). Co-occurrence of conduct disorder and its adult outcomes with depressive and anxiety disorders: A review. *Journal of the American Academy of Child and Adolescent Psychiatry, 31*, 547–556.

Index